Spiritual Leadership

Stephen Kaung

ISBN: 978-1-942521-09-9

Available from:

Christian Testimony Ministry
4424 Huguenot Road
Richmond, Virginia 23235

www.christiantestimonyministry.com

Printed in USA

Preface

The sheep are harassed and cast off because they do not have a shepherd. The harvest is there ready to be gathered, but where are the workmen? God's people are sheep, but sheep need a shepherd. Without a good shepherd the sheep will be harassed and cast away. There is great potential in God's people; but they need people who can gather them in, build them up and help them so there will be a harvest. What I feel the Lord is saying here is this: Here are the sheep, but where are the shepherds? Whether you call them shepherds, under shepherds, harvesters, reapers, workmen or any other name, there is a principle here which is of essential importance — that is the need for spiritual leadership among God's people. These messages on Spiritual Leadership were spoken by Stephen Kaung in Richmond, Virginia in 1974 and 1977. The spoken words have been transcribed by permission with only minimal editing for clarity.

Contents

1—The Need for Spiritual Leadership

Matthew 9:35-38—And Jesus went round all the cities and the villages, teaching in their synagogues, and preaching the glad tidings of the kingdom, and healing every disease and every bodily weakness. But when he saw the crowds he was moved with compassion for them, because they were harassed, and cast away as sheep not having a shepherd. Then saith he to his disciples, The harvest is great and the workmen are few; supplicate therefore the Lord of the harvest, that he send forth workmen unto his harvest.

Shall we pray:

Lord, we are before Thee; speak that Thy servants may hear. We praise and we thank Thee because Thou hast redeemed us. We are not our own. We are Thine. How we do desire that we may serve Thy purpose. We know that in ourselves there is nothing that can serve Thee; but, Lord, thou hast given Thy life to us and Thou art working in us. We pray that Thou mayest get much for Thyself among Thine own. We commit this time into Thy hands. We ask Thee to strengthen our inner man as well as our outer man that we may be able to enter into that which Thou hast for us tonight and to Thee be all the praise and the glory and the honor forever and forever. Amen.

Our Lord Jesus went around in the cities and villages and seeing the crowds that came to Him He was moved with compassion. He told His disciples that they were as sheep harassed and cast away without a shepherd and the Lord said supplicate the Lord of the harvest that he might send forth workmen to the harvest. Now, brothers and sisters, here you will find our Lord Jesus was using two parables. One is the sheep and the shepherd and the other is the harvest and the workmen. What is it that the Lord is trying to speak to His disciples?

The sheep are harassed and cast off and the reason for it is they do not have a shepherd. The harvest is there ready to be gathered, but where are the workmen? God's people are sheep, but sheep need shepherds. Without a good shepherd the sheep will be harassed and cast away. There is great potential in God's people; but you need people who can gather them in, build them up and help them so there will be a harvest. What I feel the Lord is saying here is this: Here are the sheep, but where are the shepherds? Whether you call them shepherds, under shepherds, harvesters, reapers, workmen or any other name, there is a principle here which is of essential importance and that is the need for spiritual leadership among God's people.

It is true, God's eternal purpose is the Body of Christ as we heard last night and this morning. God has an eternal purpose and He is working to have that purpose fully realized. He is the One who is working. He will never change that purpose. Sometimes we may think God is like us. When things are going a little bit hard, we try to find an easy way out. We change the course and sometimes we even quote the Scripture saying, "Does not God repent?" It is true God did repent and He does repent from time to time, but the repent there does not refer to His purpose. It only refers to His methods. He may change His method, but

8

He will never change His purpose. God's eternal purpose is that He may get a people, a flock, a body, a bride for His Son; therefore, we need to look to the Lord to open our heart and understanding to see this. Now, seeing that this is His purpose, how is God going to work towards that purpose? In His plan of operation there is one principle which is of tremendous importance and that is spiritual leadership.

Sheep are very innocent—to the extent of being ignorant. If they are left alone they cannot protect themselves. They will get into all kinds of situations of which they cannot get out. They can easily go astray and are not like dogs which can find their way home. They have to be sought after and brought back home. If the sheep do not have good shepherds, but hirelings, then when danger comes, the hirelings will flee and the sheep will be devoured. Sheep need good shepherds.

Spiritually speaking, God's people are so innocent. Thank God there is an innocence in His people. Everywhere you go you will find they are so pure to the extent of being naive. As you go around seeing God's people, you find they do have a heart for the Lord. There is nothing wrong with God's people. What is wrong is with those who lead them. In Matthew chapter 15:14 the Lord said: they are blind leaders of blind: but if blind lead blind, both will fall into a ditch.

The urgent need today among God's people is spiritual leadership. God is the God of Abraham, of Isaac, of Jacob. Now, we know His purpose was the nation of Israel, but how would He get that nation? Here you will find He gets it through Abraham, through Isaac and through Jacob. It is through the divine principle of leadership that God is able to get the nation He is after.

God's purpose was to deliver the children of Israel out of Egypt, but He had to raise up a man, Moses, to lead them out. God's purpose was to establish a kingdom on earth, to build His house that He might dwell among His people, but to arrive at that tremendous purpose, He had to raise up David and Solomon. It is true, God Himself is working out His purpose; but His way is to raise up spiritual leadership to lead the people, to help them and build them up that His purpose might be fulfilled in them. This is the direction of God's sovereign operation.

As you will find in the Book of Judges, after God had already led the people into the promised land, the Children of Israel fell away from God and He had to raise up judge after judge. When a judge was raised up, the nation returned to God and as long as the judge was living they served God, but after the judge died they immediately fell away. A little later on even when the judge was living, they began to disintegrate.

In the books of Kings and Chronicles where you see a close relationship between the kings and the people, if you have a king whose heart is perfect towards God, one that loves God, you will find the whole nation begins to turn to God. Where you had a wicked king, one that did not fear God, the result would be the falling away of the people. Leadership is of such tremendous importance.

After the children of Israel were taken into captivity you have the same thing. It was God's purpose that the people should return to Jerusalem and rebuild the temple; but in order to have that realized, God had to raise up people like Zerubbabel, Joshua, Ezra and Nehemiah. Under their leadership the people began to work with God.

When you come to the New Testament, you find the same principle working. Our Lord Jesus, while on earth, chose twelve to be His disciples and with these were the seventy and the one hundred and twenty. The Lord used these to do the work He desired to accomplish. It is true in the work of redemption our Lord Jesus was alone. He does not need our help. No one can help Him as He alone accomplishes the whole work of redemption and thank God He does. However, in the gathering of the living stones and building them up He raises up leadership to cooperate with Him in bringing what He desires into fulfilment.

It is said in Ephesians that God gave to the church some apostles, some prophets, some evangelists, some teachers and pastors for the perfecting of the saints with a view to the ministry which is the ministry of the body. God raised up elders in the church to take care of the sheep. Also in the Bible there were people called leaders, leading brethren. For instance, in Acts chapter fifteen you will remember Paul and Barnabas went to Jerusalem for that conference. The apostles and the church in Jerusalem wrote a letter to the different churches and when they sent that letter, they also sent two brethren with Paul and Barnabas. It is said:

> Then it seemed good to the apostles and to the elders, with the whole assembly, to send chosen men from among them with Paul and Barnabas to Antioch, Judas called Barnabas and Silas, leading men among the brethren. (v.22)

The leading brethren! They were not elders and yet they were leaders in the church. In other words it is not a matter of what position you occupy. It is a matter of God's divine principle of working. God must have spiritual leadership in His people in order to bring His people into His full purpose. In I Thessalonians 5:12-13 we read:

But we beg you, brethren, to know those who labor among you, and take the lead among you in the Lord, and admonish you, and to regard them exceedingly in love on account of their work.

Also, in Hebrews 13:7 we find the same thing:

Remember your leaders who have spoken to you the work of God; and considering the issue of their conversation, imitate their faith.

So brothers and sisters, I have a burden for the evening to share with you on this matter of spiritual leadership: Spiritual leadership is a must and a necessity! Without spiritual leadership God's purpose cannot be fulfilled. God is looking for spiritual leadership among His people and if He cannot find it, His work cannot be done. It is that important! How does spiritual leadership come about? It cannot be made by man. People may appoint someone to a position, but that doesn't give them spiritual leadership. It is not based upon natural talent. No matter how skilful, talented, intelligent or naturally capable you may be that does not qualify you. You may assume a position or people may put you in one, but without spiritual authority there is no spiritual leadership. Spiritual leadership comes from God and it is His choice. It is not man-made.

I would like to read you two quotations. One is not exactly a quotation, but it is a note which I took in 1957. During that year I visited England for the first time

While there our dear brother Sparks took a number of us to Scotland for a time together. Also, our brother Lance Lambert was there and that was my first time to meet our dear brother. We were spending a week or so together and each morning we came before the Lord just to wait upon

Him. During some of the mornings our brother Sparks shared with us some things which were upon his heart and one of the things he shared that impressed me very deeply at that time was on leadership. Of course, he spoke a lot on leadership, but I would like to read you just a note which I took at that time. It is not a direct quotation. It is a note which I took:

> Leadership is the direction in which divine sovereignty peculiarly works. (That's just like Mr. Sparks.)

Divine sovereignty is God Himself acting without consulting anyone. Leadership is a divine choice. True leadership bears the mark that it is something God has done. Universally speaking there is nothing to support the natural. It is a peculiar manifestation of divine sovereignty. The initiative of God is found in leadership. Men do not take the initiative. Leadership can never be of man's assumption. It must be of God. It is not professional. A leader is one who is there by the act of God.

The apostle in Latin is a man with a mandate. He has the state behind him and even if hell raises itself, he will fulfil his mission. This is the position of a leader. I think it is very clear that leadership is not something that is initiated with man. It is God's prerogative! It is God's divine sovereignty! It is an act of God! He calls, He chooses, and He puts people in leadership in the place where a person should be.

Now I would like to quote another one. I quote people who have gone before us. It is by A. W. Tozer:

> A true and safe leader is likely to be one who has no desire to lead but is forced into a position of

13

leadership by the inward pressure of the Holy Spirit and the press of the external situation.

I think that is put beautifully. He says a true and safe leader—safe leader. Moses, David and the Old Testament prophets were such leaders. I think there has hardly been a great leader from Paul to the present day; but that such a one was drafted by the Holy Spirit for the task and commissioned by the Lord of the Church to fulfil a position for which he has little heart. I believe it might be accepted as a fairly reliable rule of thumb that the man who is ambitious to lead is disqualified as a leader. Strong words; but true!

The true leader will have no desire to lord it over God's heritage; but he will be humble, gentle, self-sacrificing and altogether ready to follow as to lead when the Spirit makes it clear that a wiser and more gifted man than himself has appeared. The making of a leader, a spiritual leader, is a divine act. It is sovereign. It is not for those who are ambitious for themselves; on the contrary, you will find that God puts people into leadership in a position which they tried to avoid.

One day a brother was with St. Francis of Assisi. Probably some of you have heard of Francis of Assisi. While they were together this brother asked St. Francis:

Why thee? Why thee? Why thee? Why thee? Why is it people follow thee? Why is it people hear thee? Why is it people obey thee? You have neither beauty or intelligence nor of noble race. Why thee, why thee? It was as if he was trying to mock Francis of Assisi. Now, when St. Francis heard that, he bowed very low before the Lord and raised his eyes and entered into ecstasy. He was just full of

14

adoration and praise and after a while he turned to that brother and said: "Do you want to know, why thee, why thee? Let me tell you. The eyes of the Most High were looking upon the earth watching both the wicked and good. His eyes were trying to see if there was any sinner as small as myself. He has chosen me because I am nothing and He has chosen me to do His marvelous work to confound the wise and the noble."

Dear brothers and sisters, spiritual leadership is a necessity among God's people especially in this time when God is moving among His people and many are being awakened to Him and do have a heart for the Lord. They are seeking and searching. Yet, as you look out, it almost like our Lord Jesus when He was looking at those crowds and was moved with compassion and said they are harassed, cast off as sheep without shepherds. Oh, dear brothers and sisters, one thing we need to ask the Lord and that is: Raise up spiritual leaders—not just people who are ambitious or who are put in a position—but true leadership. God has to raise up spiritual leaders to lead His people into the realization of His full purpose.

I wonder if that isn't something which is missing today and if it isn't something about which we need to inquire of the Lord and be before Him in a very, very special way. It is true, spiritual leadership is God's divine sovereignty and choice; yet, when God chooses a person to be a leader, there is something which God has already wrought in him. We do know it is God's sovereignty and no one can assume a position of leadership; but, on the other hand, God chooses leaders because He has already worked something in that person and is able to raise them up as leaders. For one to lead he has to know the direction; therefore, it is so necessary that God find people on this earth who are open to Him and humble enough before Him to allow Him to work in them. After He has wrought His work in them, He can in turn work through them to the people.

Look at Moses. Before God could use him as a leader, He had to do His work in him. During the forty years in the wilderness he had to be reduced to absolutely nothing. Moses himself said the life span of a person is three score and ten and if it is strong, he will be four score. When God called him to that work, he was eighty years old. In other word, in his own estimate he was at his very end. God had to reduce him, empty him—empty him of his eloquence, of his might, talent, ambition, of everything of himself. God had to bring him to that point until he realizes he is but a bush—a thorn bush—ready to be consumed and yet by the grace of God he is not consumed. Even Moses forty years in Egypt was by God's sovereign arrangement.

I remember Brother sparks also said to us at that time:

> A leader is also one who not only needs to know where to lead but what to lead from.

He will be put into situations which are not for himself. Sometimes these situations seem to even be wrong and unnecessary for him and yet through such occasions he is to know the people, knowing where he will lead them out. You see, every-thing God is going to do to the people has to be wrought in him first. He is the embodiment of the work to which God is calling him.

Dear brothers and sisters, it is not just that we go out to do some work. The leadership work to which God is calling you is already being done in you. You are not a stranger to that. You have allowed God to make you acquainted with the whole situation in principle and because of that He is able to entrust you with leadership. Otherwise it would be the blind leading the blind. Spiritual leadership is a very costly thing during the process. It is costly both in the leadership position and in the making of a leader.

John Bunyan's Grace Abounding is actually his autobiography. I think we read mostly Pilgrim's Progress; but in this book he tells us of some of his experiences. Sometimes you wonder why it is so difficult for John Bunyan to get saved. He did have a desire to be saved. Some people do not have this and God saves them. Here he was very anxious to be saved and yet salvation seemed to evade him. Oh, he went through times of depression, difficult times and he was still not saved. Sometimes you wonder: Is it necessary? Thank God, because John Bunyan went through all these things the result was he was able to help people into the way of salvation.

A leader is one in whom God has to do some work more than anyone else. Are you willing to let God do such a work? We often think of leadership as a very glorious thing. Oh how we long to be leaders. Among the twelve disciples there was the constant fight: Who was the leader. Everyone of them wanted to be the first. Even at the very last (when our Lord Jesus was in Jerusalem for the last time) the two sons of Zebedee got their mother involved asking our Lord to let one sit on the right and the other on the left in positions of importance of leadership. The Lord said, Among the nations the leaders, the kings lord it over the other people, but this is not so among you. If you want to be the first, you must be the smallest. Also, the Son of man came to serve and not to be served and to give His life a ransom for many.

Dear brothers and sisters, for the sake of God's purpose, for the sake of God's people, we need to so commit and give ourselves to the Lord that we will allow Him to work everything He wants in us. Unless we have such a heart, God is not able to use us as leaders.

Again, leadership is not based upon the natural. Some people are born leaders. It is natural for them to lead, but that is a very dangerous things. God either has to set them aside completely or He has to deal with them so drastically that they are reduced to nothing before He can really use them as leaders. Do not think that because you are not a natural-born leader therefore God will not choose you. God always surprises us. We are talking about true leadership and about the true work of God. We are not talking about such work as the people in this world will recognize; but we are speaking about how God's purpose can be accomplished. Again, it is God Himself who works; but He works through the leadership.

How does leadership come about? It is by the way of discipleship. If a person is not willing to follow, he is not fit to lead. The Lord said if anyone desired to follow Him, then let him deny himself and take up his cross and follow Him. If we are not ready to follow the Lord wherever He goes, we are not fit to lead.

One day someone came up to the Lord and said: Lord, I want to follow you. He was a scribe. The Lord said: Do you know what it means? The birds have nests; the foxes have holes; but the Son of man has no where to lay His head.

Brothers and sisters, are we committed to the Lord? Do not think first of leadership. Think first of discipleship. Are you a true disciple of the Lord? Have you committed your life to the Lord in such a way that He is able to break you, mold you and make you as it pleases Him? Are you that committed to Him?

Of course, the word "disciple" cannot be separated from the word "discipline." A disciple's life is a disciplined one. As we commit ourselves into the hand of our Lord, we leave it to Him to discipline us. Dear brothers and sisters, this is the way to leadership. Are we ready for it? Many aspire for leadership; but few are willing to be disciples of the Lord. As a matter of fact, there is only One in the whole universe who is fit to lead. None of us is fit. God has raised up one leader. You remember it is said: Look off unto Jesus, the leader and completer of our faith. Only our Lord Jesus is fit to lead. Why? Because He has learned obedience from the things which He suffered. Even though He was equal with God, and it is not something to be grasped, yet He emptied Himself, took upon Himself the form of a slave and being in the likeness of a man He further humbled Himself before God being obedient unto the Father, even unto death, and that the death of the cross. Brothers and sisters, when our Lord Jesus came to this earth to be a man, He followed the Father completely—every step of His way—even unto death, the death of the cross. Because of that God has made Him the leader.

Spiritual leadership is in Christ. If anyone should say: "I am going to lead. I am able to lead. I am a leader." he disqualifies himself. It is Christ in you who leads. If it is not Christ, then you mislead the people. Dear brothers and sisters, how we have misled God's people. We think we know. We think we are in a position to lead. We are ambitious thinking we are capable. We try to lead and both fall into ditches. I think we need to realize one thing which is: We are not fit to lead. We must learn to follow—follow the Lord.

It is the Lord in you who leads. Now, how is this so? Again, you will find that is a mystery. It is the Lord in you who leads and yet He leads in you and through you. Outwardly it looks as if you are leading, but actually it is not. By the Holy Spirit the Lord Himself is being organized and wrought in you. god has not only made known His mind to you, but He has also worked in you to such an extent that He has a place in you. That is spiritual authority and that is spiritual leadership.

Let's look into the life of Paul. Here is a man whom God raised up and of all those who have been used certainly Paul was one of the greatest instruments in His hand for the purpose of God concerning His people. Paul was a master builder and how God used him to build that spiritual house. He was certainly a great leader. God gave him such leadership for the body of Christ; but dear brothers and sisters, everything for which he was used towards bringing the people into the realization of the body of Christ was first wrought in him. Before his conversion he was a great man—the Pharisee. Paul was not an unknown person. He was born in Tarsus, reared and educated in Jerusalem under the feet of Gamaliel, the great teacher. He was a Pharisee of the Pharisees.

This man Saul was such a person, not only learned, but he had a dynamic personality. We are told by tradition that Saul was very small in stature and yet he was a dynamic person and had such a driving force. He did such havoc to the believers in the beginning, but one day....God met him on the road to Damascus and reduced him to nothing. He met the Lord! Never before did Saul acknowledge that anyone was greater than himself. He felt that he must lead, but now he says: "Lord, who are you? What shall I do?" His whole life was surrendered to the Lord. He allowed the Lord to work in him so greatly that Christ had such a place in his life that whatever Christ had worked in him then that was his authority. That was his ministry and that was his leadership. It was not Paul.

Strangely enough, I do not know who gave him the name Paul; but, you know Paul means "little." So far as he was concerned, he was no longer Saul, that great man, he was Paul—little. He even said he was chief of sinners, less than the least of all the saints and yet, dear brothers and sisters, there is no doubt there is spiritual leadership in that man. He said, "Imitate me as I have imitated Christ." Oh, how he followed Christ, how he was discipled to Christ, how he allowed Christ to break him and make him.

Paul said, "Not I but Christ. I bear in my body the dying of Jesus. I die daily that the life of Jesus may be manifested in me and in you." That is spiritual leadership.

Dear brothers and sisters, may we be before the Lord as I feel this is something of urgent need today among God's people. Let us cry unto the Lord to raise up spiritual leaders—true leaders in whom God has already wrought the work which He wants to fulfil.

Also, may we be before the Lord tonight and say:

> Lord, we are in Thy hand. We do not choose this, We do not try to get it; but, we are here in Your hand. Whatever You want, have Your way.

May we really take some time for prayer and pour out this burden before the Lord. Ask the Lord of the harvest to raise up spiritual leaders for the need of His purpose and His people today.

2—Qualifications For Spiritual Leadership

John 15:5—I am the vine, ye are the branches. He that abides in me and I in him, he bears much fruit; for without me ye can do nothing.

John 15:16—Ye have not chosen me, but I have chosen you, and have set you that ye should go and that ye should bear fruit, and that your fruit should abide, that whatsoever ye ask the Father in my name he may give you.

In our previous message we mentioned that the Lord is looking for men that can be spiritual leaders among His own people. God's purpose is to gather to Himself a people—a people who will be His Bride, the Bride of the Lamb. In order to arrive at that purpose in God's working there is a divine principle. This spiritual leadership is not something that comes from man nor is it established by man. It must come from God for it is divine sovereignty.

The Bible says, "Ye have not chosen me, but I have chosen you..." In the case of spiritual leadership it is purely God's choice. He chooses those whom He has prepared, those who have allowed Him to do a certain work in their lives. So, dear brothers and sisters, as we see God working on this earth today awakening His people everywhere, we should in-quire of Him for the raising up of spiritual leaders to give to the Church. Also, knowing that spiritual leadership is not based on anything natural we should allow Him to complete His work in us. If He desires to use us, let us lay our-selves before Him. I do believe this is an urgent need among God's people today.

In order to have spiritual leadership we must first be willing to be disciples of our Lord Jesus since this comes from discipleship. Unless we are willing to follow we are not fit to lead!

Let us now consider some of the qualities God is looking for in leaders. Of course, there are a great number of qualities that constitute spiritual leaders; but for our fellowship this evening we will just mention a few as examples.

Spirituality is a must. Now this is very evident because God is not looking for leadership in the things of this world. If you are looking for that, you will have to find those with a dynamic personality, a very strong will, a big mind, gifts, talents, great administrative ability, good solid background, good training, good connections, etc.

Now these are the essentials for leadership in the things of this world; but God is not looking for these. He is looking for spirituality or if you want you may use the term "maturity." What is spirituality? It is not that you have a great deal of knowledge or have accumulated a lot of religious information. Spirituality is a matter of the measure of Christ in you. God is looking for a secret, hidden life with himself. spiritual leadership is based upon a history with the Lord. This is not an instant thing. In this country we like for everything to be instant—instant coffee and tea. We are so impatient. Even in spiritual things we are always trying to find ways to be an instant spiritual person. But dear brothers and sisters, the way to spiritual leadership is through a secret, hidden life with the Lord. In secret He is preparing this leadership and working Himself into that per-son. When the time comes, God will reveal and manifest that leadership. For instance in the life of David we have this incident:

Before he appeared before the children of Israel, he was almost unknown. He was the youngest in the family and his father did not think too much of him. His elder brothers misunderstood him a great deal and actually looked down upon him. He was sent out to the field to tend a few sheep, but this shepherding became more than just that. Here he had real experience with God Himself in a secret and hidden way. No one knew about this—not even his family.

There was only one who noticed David—a young man who stood before King Saul when he had problems and said: "I have seen this young man the son of Jesse. He is a mighty man of God and he plays beautiful music." Now when David was sent by his father to the battlefield to see about his brothers, he found everyone afraid. So he offered to go and fight this Philistine giant. King Saul began to inquire after him to find out his background asking him how he knew he could go out and fight this Philistine and what training he had had. Here David related to him his life with the Lord. As he was tending sheep he learned to know God in the most practical way. When the bear and lion would come, David by the strength of the Lord could tear the lion apart delivering the sheep out of its mouth. He said if God can deliver me from the paws of the lion and the bear certainly He can deliver me from the hands of this Philistine.

The Lord is looking for spiritual leaders and it is not a matter of aspiration or ambition. These people are already disqualified; but, for the sake of the Lord, His Church and for His purpose to be realized, oh, brothers and sisters, how we need to be before the Lord that we might have this secret, hidden life with Him. This will be done in our daily life in the very small things. These are the ways whereby we learn to know the Lord. It is here that God will test us, deal with us until He can get the quality of leadership He de-sires. How often we are looking for great experiences. How often we think that if God is going to raise up a leader then He has to lead him through spectacular experiences; but it is in the little things of our daily living that God trains us and works out His purpose.

What is spirituality? It is Christ being known, apprehended and experienced. It is Christ who fills our being. Oh, brothers and sisters, this is true spirituality and this comes from the Holy Spirit. The very word "Spirit" connects us with the Spirit of God. A person who lives in the spirit is not one that lives in the flesh. One who does live in the flesh cannot suddenly become a spiritual leader. No, for a person to be a spiritual leader he has to be one who lives in the spirit and under the Holy Spirit.

As you read the book of Acts you will find God raised up many leaders. No matter what the position was whether apostles, deacons, service tables or looking after the widows, the one qualification was "full of the Holy Spirit." Now there may be other things to be considered such as an honest, good life, good testimony before the world, not double tongued etc., but above all these is to be spirit filled. What does this mean? Brothers and sisters, do forgive me for saying this but I often meet people who say this person is spirit filled. Now in the mind of most when we mention that these people are spirit filled, it means once upon a time they had an experience of the Holy Spirit. This was maybe five or ten years ago and certainly at that time they were spirit filled. Let's look at this word in Ephesians 5:18.

And be not drunk with wine, in which is debauchery; but be filled with the Spirit.

Now all who have been born again have the Holy Spirit within. He comes into our new spirit to dwell there making all things new and He bears witness with our spirit that we are children of God. Who is this one? He is the diving person. He is the Another Comforter. He is God Himself dwelling in our spirit giving comfort, strength and everything else we need. But the problem today with God's people is not whether you have the Holy Spirit, it is: Are you filled with Him? To be filled with the Holy Spirit and to possess Him are very different. You have the Holy Spirit and you may be using Him; but to be filled with Him is to let Him use you.

To be filled with the Holy Spirit means you have surrendered your life to the Lord and have so given yourself to Him that He has full charge. In other words you have handed yourself to the Spirit of God to be under His full control. Being full of the Holy Spirit speaks of a state not just an experience. We may have an experience and that comes and goes; but a state is something that continues. If you abandon yourself to the Lord completely, the Holy Spirit will come into your life taking full charge guiding and leading you in everything He deems necessary to incorporate and organize Christ in you. As He is doing this in us this state needs to be maintained day after day. Because you were filled with the spirit yesterday doesn't mean you are filled today.

I John 1:7—But if we walk in the light as he is in the light, we have fellowship with one another, and the blood of Jesus Christ his Son cleanses us from all sin.

Now as God's light in you begins to shine and you walk in that light of life, then He fills you. You are supplied and filled for that day; but if tomorrow God's life in you has grown a little bit larger and there is a greater light of life shining upon your path and you are disobedient and do not corporate, then, even though you were filled yesterday, you are yet to be filled today. It is a daily thing with the Lord. Dear brothers and sisters, true spirituality comes from a life completely given to the Lord and governed by the Holy Spirit. The Holy Spirit in you has an important work to do and that is to form Christ in you. We do have Christ but He has to be formed in you and in the measure of the formation of Christ in you that is the measure of true spirituality. It is only in how much He is increased and matured in you that God will use you as leaders for His people. John the Baptist said, "He must increase and I must decrease" and this is the way to spirituality. So, dear brothers and sisters, the first quality that God is looking for and which must be in a spiritual leader is spirituality.

Vision is another must for spiritual leaders. He should be one who sees. If he does not have vision, then it is the blind leading the blind.

By vision it does not mean you have to see something physically. Of course, even today God is able to give people physical vision—no doubt about that—but that is not the point. Vision means that God unveils His mind to you. He unveils His heart and reveals to you the purpose He has purposed in Christ Jesus. By vision we do not mean here a little and there a little.

In other words, every Christian must have seen something and as you go on with the Lord, certainly He will show you things. Now, some people say things like this:

This morning as I was reading the Bible I saw something. Oh, I am so happy that I saw this. There was a passage in the Scripture that always puzzled me but suddenly I have light and I now begin to see it. I know how to explain that verse.

We do thank God if He gives light on some passages. We thank Him for that; but dear brothers and sisters, a spiritual leader needs to have a clear and comprehensive vision, not just a little bit here and there. To put it in another way, it is the vision which Saul saw on the road to Damascus. Paul, towards the end of his life, could stand before the judge and the people and say, "I was not disobedient to the heavenly vision" (Acts 26:19). He was a person who had caught a vision and that vision had caught him. His whole life afterwards was to obey that vision. Today God's people so need leaders who have really been given a vision by the Lord—a vision of what is really in His mind and that controls the working of God from one eternity to another eternity.

Do you see what God is after? Is it that God is just after you as an individual person? Of course, He is highly interested in you; but have you seen that God has something far greater? As our brother has been telling us in these few sessions, God has a wonderful, marvelous purpose and He desires to involve you in it. His purpose is that Christ's body may be matured and built up. God has made Him Head over all things to the body. When His body has been built up, He will come back to claim that very body to be His Bride. Brothers and sisters, this is a vision that we must see, and it is not something that you mentally grasp. It comes from revelation. Are you caught up with that vision?

29

Also, a person who has a vision has a burden. Look at the prophets. Oftentimes you will find it said:

"The burden of the Lord is upon me." Now, where comes such burden? Why are some people burdened and others not? Things happen on this earth and some people are burdened before the Lord. Others see this same thing yet do not have the burden. Why? Be-cause those who do see are seeing what is beyond that which is visible and are looking into the very purpose and mind of God. When you see it like this, you get a burden and you can't get away from it.

Last night I mentioned being with brother Sparks in 1957 and his talking to us about leadership. He said another thing. Notice this:

> Leadership is not based on ambition. It is based on distress!

It is not because you are ambitious or want to be in that position or seek after it that you will get the leadership. It is quite the contrary. Leadership comes by distress. You are deeply distressed and because you are so burdened before the Lord, you lay yourself before Him seeking and inquiring after Him and then He says, "Go."

Look at Nehemiah who was the king's cupbearer even though he was actually a captive. This position was very high in the king's court. It was not just a waiter in the modern sense. The cupbearer was the king's most intimate friend. Why? Because in those days there were despots and the kings always feared someone would like to take their life. There-fore when the king would drink or eat, he needed to make sure there was no poison. But who could they trust? The cup-bearer was one who was the closest to the king, his friend and confidant. Before the cupbearer would hand him the cup he would drink it first. The king trusted his life to the cupbearer and the cupbearer was willing to sacrifice his life for the king. If there was poison he would die. Now Nehemiah being in such a position was certainly trusted by the king and lived a life of comfort and luxury; yet he was concerned for his brethren who were in Jerusalem.

When his own brother and several others came back from Jerusalem they brought the news to him that the people in Jerusalem were in great affliction and under great reproach. Why? Because the wall was broken; there was no gate; they were exposed to the enemy and had absolutely no protection or defense. They were just trodden down and if they remained in this state, they might be completely annihilated for many had left and returned to captivity. The Bible says when Nehemiah heard this he wept before the Lord, he fasted before the Lord, he fell down before the Lord! He was deeply distressed and looked to the Lord to open a way for him and God sent him back to rebuild the wall of Jerusalem. Here is a man in distress!

Dear brothers and sisters, are you ever in distress? Oh, yes, we are in distress for ourselves all the time. In any little discomfort or little thing that may not satisfy us we immediately complain and murmur. But who are those that are distressed and why? They are ones who have seen that God did not have His desire among His people. In seeing that His people afar short of the glory of God they are so jealous for Him to be satisfied. Now how does one in distress solve this problem? He cannot be passive and shake his head and say, "Too bad, too bad, what can I do?" When one is distressed because of the vision God has given him, there is no way out but to go to the Lord and inquire.

Oh, brothers and sisters, what the Church needs today are leaders—those who are distressed because of the vision God has given them that they cannot help it. Some people say: "Why are you so dissatisfied? Isn't everything all right?" The Church at Laodicea said: "We are fine—so rich- -lacking nothing. Why is it you always say something is wrong and always in distress?" Oh, if you catch a vision of the Lord, seeing what He wants to have among His people for His Beloved Son and all that Christ has given Himself for, you cannot help it.

It is not that you just have a complaining, murmur-ing character and are never satisfied. There is the contentment in the Lord; that is true; but if God has given you a vision, there is no way out. You have to be before the Lord until that burden is discharged.

Do not think that those who have vision have a good time. If you want to have a good time, close your eyes. If the Lord should open your eyes to see His heart and mind, you cannot rest any more. It is just like David when he said he could not allow his eyes to sleep or give slumber to his eyelids. Why? Because there was a burden in his heart to build God a house, to find a place for the ark. Do you have a vision from the Lord? When the Lord apprehends a person by showing him what He desires, he will have a very difficult time. Remember the prophet Jeremiah saying these things:

> I am going to give up. I will not continue. I have not chosen this. It is something put on me by you. I cannot bear it and I don't want to see anything else. I will close my ears and shut my eyes. I am going to close my mouth and speak no more as though I have not seen.

Now, if you will notice in the Scripture where he said he would speak of him no more, it also says, "but it was in my heart as a burning fire shut up in my bones; and I became wearied with holding in, and I could not" (Jeremiah 20:9). He could not help it and this is leadership. He got a man- date from God.

Oh, brothers and sisters, we need vision because through vision we get burden and with burden we get distress and this is the quality of leadership.

Brokenness is another quality God is looking for in a spiritual leader or if you like you may say humility because it comes from brokenness.

Naturally speaking we are not humble. the most humble person can be the proudest. You know this country seems to rub other nations the wrong way and yet they supply food and aid to them. Why is this so? Because the poorest nation is the proudest. You touch their pride. Don't think you are humble for when you say you are, that is the proudest sign. Look at Christ—the spirit of Christ is the spirit of humility. But humility is not natural; it comes from brokenness. God has no need for a person who is perfect in himself. The only vessel He can use is a broken one.

We have this treasure in earthen vessels and thank God for this treasure. The treasure is Christ and we are but the earthen vessel. You know the earthen vessel is of such a nature that it does not allow the radiancy of the treasure to come forth. It is hidden. If you desire to have the radiancy and brilliancy of the treasure shine, there is only one way: The vessel must be broken.

Brothers and sisters, when you meet people what do they touch? Is it your cleverness, your knowledge, your ability, your energy? Is it you? Now if that is so and you impress and impart nothing but the earthen vessel, then how can people be built up spiritually? There is only one way in which people can meet Christ in you and in which you can minister life to them and that is this vessel must be a broken one.

Self preservation is a human instinct. We all like to keep ourselves intact; but our Lord said we must lay down our lives by denying ourselves, taking up the cross and following Him. This simply means being broken—being broken before Him. An illustration of brokenness is in the case of Moses.

In the Egyptian palace where he was trained, he was mighty in word and deed—a great man, intact, perfect, complete in himself. He had a sense of destiny feeling God had raised him up to deliver His people. On the basis of that when he was 40 years old, he went out to see his Hebrew brethren who were slaves at that time. When he looked at things he saw an Egyptian evilly treating a Hebrew. He beat the Egyptian to death and buried him in the sand. The next day he saw two Hebrew brothers fighting and became involved in that asking them not to fight as they were brothers. They said, "Who are you? Who has made you our leader?"

Now Moses fully thought they knew God had raised him up as their leader; but they didn't. This was a surprise to Moses. Why was it God could not use him at that time? It was because he was too perfect, too intact, too complete and thought too much of himself; so God had to break him. After being rejected by his brethren he had to flee for his life to the wilderness for forty years. This was not a short period of time and he must have gone over that scene in his mind many times trying to find out what went wrong until he dis-covered it went wrong right in him. Yes, right in him! God used forty years to undo him, to finish him, to

34

break him, to shatter him. He lost his ambition, his eloquence and his might. In fact, he lost everything and came to the end of himself even expecting God not to use him. Now, it was at that very point that God raised him up as a leader to the children of Israel.

You know, the Bible says Moses was the meekest of all men; but I don't think we get that impression when we see an artist's picture of him. they paint him so masculine to the point of being violent and he is portrayed as such a law giver, so serious, so strict and so harsh. Now humility does not mean weakness. It is strength and because of that strength you can afford to be humble. Most people cannot afford to be humble because they have nothing left; but here, because God had broken him, we see him leading the children of Israel through the wilderness with their murmuring and even his own brother and sister criticizing him. What did he do when he was faced with all of these things? He fell upon his face before the Lord. Oftentimes it is the thing in which God works the most in a person that he will be tested in and we know that Moses could not enter the promised land because just once he lost his temper calling the children of Israel "rebels" saying, "...shall we bring forth to you water out of this rock?" (Numbers 20:10).

On all the other occasions Moses was the humblest person you could ever have. He was their leader and yet you can kick and push him. He would say, "You don't push me far enough. I will lie down." You cannot touch him. We do thank God, though he was not able to enter the promised land, he was on the Mount of Transfiguration. Dear brothers and sisters, brokenness is a quality of leadership and sad to say, we do not see much in so-called leaders.

Inspiring others is also something a leader should be able to do.

Since you as a leader have caught a vision and been burdened and distressed before the Lord, you need to discharge and fulfill it. It is something you can never do by your- self. You have to inspire the people of God with that vision which God has given you. You have to share this burden and in a sense you make them distressful too. Otherwise you will never be able to fulfill your leadership. How can a general go to the battlefield and fight if his soldiers do not follow him? One of the best illustrations in the Old Testament is the prophetess Deborah. This was at a time when the children of Israel were in such a low state being oppressed by the Canaanites and God raised up a judge in a woman, Deborah the prophetess. Why didn't He raise up a man? Shame to the men!

There wasn't any. Here we see that Deborah didn't just do it herself. She inspired Barak. Deborah represented the divine principle of inspiration.

Dear brothers and sisters, who is a leader among God's people? Not the one who does it all by himself; but he is one who can inspire others getting them to work with him. Oftentimes, especially in the Church, you may see something which probably others have not and something needs to be done. Oh, how easy it would be to just go ahead and do it and be finished. You may be able to do it even better than others; but the principle of God's working in the Church is corporateness. Yes, God raises up leaders but not those who monopolize doing everything for the people. These leaders are raised up by God that they might see further, inspiring God's people and bringing them in to work.

Nehemiah had a burden concerning the condition of the wall of Jerusalem and in the night he went out with a few to look at this wall which was ruined and broken down. In a sense he was ~alone; but the next day he gathered the people and inspired them, burdened them and they gathered together as one man to build the wall of Jerusalem. The Word tells us that particular families built certain sections until the whole wall was connected and finished. A leader is one who can inspire and lead others; but the people are doing that work.

Also, in this connection there must be the working together with the people and not being individualistic or independent. You cannot have the notion that since you are a leader you can be independent. No! Fellowship is the principle of the body. God raised you as leaders but you need to fellow-ship with the brothers and sisters. There must be a working together.

Why is it in the Church the elderhood is always plural in number? We would think if there would be just one elder that would be the simplest way to govern; but God decided there would be the elderhood. Even among them there is a divine order; yet not in the sense of a presiding elder by vote. Why? Because the working of the body of Christ is following the principle of fellowship. Through the fellowship of the elders coming into one mind and one spirit on matters there is not just a deciding of everything and ordering the brothers and sisters to carry them out. Not so. Even before they come to the decision before the Lord, they try to find out the feeling of the body being open to fellowship with the brothers and sisters in the Church. There is an openness between the elders and the brothers and sisters and when they allow the people to fellowship, then they bring everything before the Lord so that the mind of the Spirit may be known. There must be coordination and cooperation.

A leader is a person who is able to work together with all the brothers and sisters and the other leaders whom God has raised up. It is true this sometimes becomes very trouble-some and it seems many things have to wait. It may look like a waste of time; but eventually you will find there is great blessing in it. The unity of God's people must be kept with all diligence. In summary we would say a leader is not just a person who rules over everything, deciding all and doing it by himself; but is able to inspire and work with others. Again, let us emphasize, it is not something naturally in us. Rather, it is the Holy Spirit working Christ in us.

It is CHRIST who is true spirituality.
It is CHRIST who is brokenness.
It is CHRIST who is the vision.
It is CHRIST who is the burden and distress.
It is CHRIST who is the enabler.

I would like to mention one last thing and that is the cost of leadership. When God is making a leader it costs a lot; but after you are called into spiritual leadership it doesn't mean that from now on it's all prize and no cost. No! When God puts a person in the position of leadership, it is very, very costly.

Remember the two disciples James and John who came to the Lord with their mother asking Him to promise whatever they would ask He would give. They wanted Him to sign a blank check; but we know our Lord never signs such a check. In-stead He says, "What do you want?" Their mother requests that one sit on the right and the other on His left. Our Lord replies: "Ye know not what ye ask. Can you drink the cup which I am about to drink, or be baptized with the baptism that I am baptized with?" They do not really know what the cup and baptism mean; but they are so anxious to be on the right and left that they will promise anything. They respond, "Yes, we are able." The Lord says, "Yes, you will; whether you like it or not; but to sit on my right and left is not for me to give but for my Father who is in heaven."

What does all this mean? It means that to be in leadership is costly. You have to drink the cup the Lord drinks and be baptized with the baptism with which He is. When did He drink the cup? In the Garden of Gethsemane. When was the Lord baptized with the baptism that He was baptized with? On Calvary's cross. In other words, to be a true leader you must lay down your life. The Lord said He laid down His life for us and we ought to lay down our lives for one another.

One day someone asked a great man how much did it cost to build up such an empire and his answer was: "Not very much—just one's own life-blood! That's all." Dear brothers and sisters, the cost of leadership is your very life. You have to lay down your life for the brothers and sisters and the vision which God has given you. It demands your life! If you are not willing for this, don't be a leader. Paul said, "I bear in my body the dying of Jesus that the life of Jesus may be manifested in you. I die daily." It is nothing less than that and it is not a sudden thing.

Oh, brothers and sisters, people say, "If only I can die a martyr's death, then I will get a martyr's crown right away." But, unfortunately, there is no persecution here. If we do not live a martyr's life, how can we die a martyr's death? The Bible says we are a living sacrifice. That is a martyr's life. What is a sacrifice? It is something that is offered on the altar to be consumed slowly but surely until it is reduced to ashes and the smoke rises as a sweet smelling savor. The Bible says it is the food of God—a living sacrifice. If this is the cost for every brother and sister, then how much more will it demand of the leaders. Peter said the elders are shepherds of the flock and are not to lord it over them but should set an example for them. Leadership is costly—it costs you your very blood and life.

Leadership is very lonely. It is true, in one sense, you have the brothers and sisters with you; yet in another way you are the loneliest person in the world. Even the people do not know and understand. You stand alone with God and you have to learn to bear this loneliness. It is not that you do not want to be friends or have a good time. Other people may but you cannot. God's dealings with you will be severe and very strict, more than any other people and that puts you in a lonely position; but if you have the vision there is no escape.

A leader is a person that will be criticized. Very few are appreciated when they are living. Someone has said:

> A leader is one for whom people will build a monument after he dies with the stones which they threw at him.

That is the cost of leadership; but dear brothers and sisters, take heart. It is worth it for the Lord.

What are some of the dangers and perils of leadership: I believe pride is number one. Look at Saul. Before he was put in the position of leadership he seemed to be humble. When Samuel disclosed to him that God had chosen him to be the King of Israel, he said, "No, no! I am the smallest of the tribes of Israel and the smallest in my family. Who am I to be that leader?" As Samuel gathered all the people to choose from them a leader, they cast lots and when they took out the name of Saul, they couldn't find him. He hid himself among his baggage. He seemed to be very humble; but, oh, when he ascended to the throne of Israel, that which was really himself began to emerge. The cross had not worked in that life. His humbleness was false. Saul began to be a proud king wanting everything for himself. His face was more important than anything else. Pride is the number one danger of leadership.

Another thing, when God begins to use a person and pros-pers him, the danger is that he can become ambitious. He might not be that way in the beginning because that would disqualify him. He has no desire to be in the place of leadership but after he is put there, he begins to see God using him and he likes that. He will begin to build a kingdom for himself instead of doing the work of God saying, "This is my work. This is what I have done."

I remember my brother who was a general contractor. He got up very early in the morning going to build houses in the city of Shanghai and other cities. He told me the one thing that comforted him above all things was when he was driving around in the city, he could say, "Now, this place I built." That was his comfort. Why? It is his kingdom. Dear brothers and sisters, leadership can turn into such a hideous thing and you can be just building a kingdom for yourself. You become ambitious.

Also, in this connection you begin to look for success. Who does not want success? But is it success you are seeking or God's approval? When he is looking for success and God does not bless certain things, he tries to make it seem like a blessing. He has to make it successful. If it does not come from the Holy Spirit, then he has to supply it for

Him because he cannot afford to fail. Oh, this a great temptation to leadership.

Another danger to be considered is jealousy. When he looks around and sees God has used others more than he, he begins to be jealous. If you are not in a position of leadership, you do not get jealous very easily. That is why you will find jealousies among leaders. I often say God's people are so good—nothing wrong with God's people. If you find any problem, it rests with the leaders.

Popularity is something else that tempts leaders. You begin to seek to be popular and because of that you have to compromise. Or you will go to the other extreme. You feel yourself so important that you become infallible. Everybody else can be wrong but you cannot!

Generally speaking these are the dangers of leadership. Now, if God raises up people to be leaders, let us not draw back. Do not push yourself into leadership; but neither should you draw back. When God called Moses to leadership he drew back not wanting to go and you remember God was angry. Why? Because he was not thinking of God but of himself.

Dear brothers and sisters, what are the consolations of leadership? One is as Paul said to the church at Philippi: If I may be poured forth with you on your sacrifice, I rejoice. Oh, if only God's people can see and be built together; if only they can be offered to God, if it requires you to be poured forth as a drink offering, then rejoice. That is your joy and your crown. Also, when the Lord shall return, He will say, "Well done, good and faithful servant. You are faithful in little things; I am going to give you many things. Enter into the joy of the Lord." If the Lord should have it, that is all that matters.

So, dear brothers and sisters, let us look to the Lord. Oh, spiritual leadership is so much needed today among God's people.

3—Spiritual Leadership—King Asa

II Chronicles:16:9—For the eyes of Jehovah run to and fro through the whole earth, to shew himself strong in the behalf of those whose heart is perfect toward him ...

Before we get into what we would like to fellowship on this evening, I believe it would be helpful if we could make some general observations on the two books of Chronicles. Sometimes we may think Chronicles is a repetition of Kings; but if you read carefully, you will find the two books of Chronicles are very different from the two books of Kings. In Chronicles the Spirit of God gives us only the record of King David and his successor Solomon and the kings of the nation of Judah. Furthermore, it is not just a record of the kings of the nation of Judah; but they are given with a very specific viewpoint which is in relation to the covenant and the worship of God. Wherever you find there are kings faithful to God's covenant and who restore God's word, that nation will be blessed and in rest and prosperity. However, should kings violate the covenant and corrupt God's worship, that nation will be cursed and in ruins.

God puts great emphasis on leadership. The kings are leaders and the people are like sheep. As you know, the sheep depend very much on the shepherd. If there is a good shepherd, then the flock will really prosper and be blessed; but if there is a bad shepherd, then woe to the sheep because they cannot protect themselves. They do not know the way and are so innocent to the point of ignorance and weakness.

You know, in a sense, this principle of spiritual leadership is applicable even in our day. It is true everyone is responsible directly to God and we can never put the blame on someone else as we have the Holy Spirit in us that we might know the mind of Christ. If in any way we are mislead, we, too, are responsible because we have the Holy Spirit in us. Yet, on the other hand, the leaders who are raised up by God have tremendous responsibility because God holds them responsible not only for what they are and do, but for the people that are put in their care.

When our Lord Jesus was on earth, He looked upon this matter of leadership as one of tremendous importance. You remember He said: "Leave them alone; they are blind leaders of blind: but if blind lead blind, both will fall into a ditch" (Matthew 15:14). In Matthew, chapter 23, we see our Lord Jesus denouncing the leaders of His day, proclaiming woes over them. Why? Because God held them responsible for His people.

So, as we look into the two books of Chronicles, we will learn much about spiritual leadership—its place, its responsibility and effect upon the whole nation. Also, we shall see how God is faithful to His promise, His covenant with David. Again and again, because God was mindful of His covenant with David, you will find God would not completely destroy the house of David so that there might be a lamp in his house. Even though there were many wicked kings in the nation of Judah, yet God was so reluctant to remove the lampstand. Unfortunately, towards the end there was nothing God could do but remove it and the nation of Judah was taken into Babylonian captivity.

Now in the spiritual application there is a difference. If we take the nation of Judah as a type of the Church which is supposed to be a lampstand shining for the testimony of Jesus in this dark world, we see the Church has failed in fulfilling her mission. But God is faithful and throughout the centuries, even in the darkest hours of Church history, there has never failed to be a lamp somewhere. Men may fail; the Church in general may fail; but God's testimony continues on. There is a lamp there—always shining! And, it is because of the faithfulness of God. The Lord has said:

> Zechariah 12:8—In that day will Jehovah defend the inhabitants of Jerusalem; and he that stumbleth among them at that day shall be as David; and the house of David as God, as the Angel of Jehovah before them.

Here is the difference: In the history of the nation of Judah the lamp was extinguished for a long time until it was restored in the Son of David, Christ. But in the history of the Church Christ is so faithful that He maintains that lamp throughout the centuries through the house of David, that is the company of overcomers. So the principle of overcomers can be found in the two books of Chronicles. Having seen these things, we would like to fellowship on one of the kings of Judah.

Unfortunately, there were more wicked than good kings; but thank God for those who were good. God raised up a number of good kings in the nation of Judah; such as Asa, Jehoshaphat, Hezekiah and Josiah. God, in His great love towards His people, raised up good leadership and through them the nation was blessed. This evening we will just fellowship on King Asa.

47

The account of King Asa can be found in 2 Chronicles chapters 14 through 16. We could not read all these chapters so I hope you will read them afterwards. Now, Asa was the grandson of Rehoboam, the son of Solomon. You know, under Rehoboam the nation was divided into the northern kingdom of ten tribes and the southern kingdom of two tribes. Rehoboam ruled over the southern kingdom, the nation of Judah and he was a wicked king who had no heart for God. After him was Abijah who had a little heart for God and then came Asa of whom is said:

> And Asa did what was good and right in the sight of Jehovah his God ... (II Chronicles 14:2)

The grandfather was wicked; the father had little heart for the Lord; but the grandson, Asa, seemed to have much heart for God. He did what was good and right in the sight of the Lord. He took away the altars of the strange god and the high places. He broke down the columns and cut down the Asherahs. These are the things and the places of idol worship. He also commanded Judah to seek Jehovah the God of their fathers and to practice the law and the commandments. Negatively he got rid of the abominations which were contradictory to the worship of the God of their fathers. Positively he commanded the people to seek the Lord. Because he was in a position of leadership, he was able to lead the people in this way and there was rest in the land for ten years. There was no war and during this time of rest there was much building going on. You know, dear brothers and sisters, if we set our hearts to seek the Lord and do what is good and right in the sight of God getting rid of anything which is contradictory to the worship of God, what will happen? Two things will be the result: First, we will have rest and second, there will be building going on.

In Matthew chapter 11 our Lord Jesus said: "Come to me all ye that labor and are heavy laden and I will give you rest." Before we came to the Lord, we were laboring and heavily laden. We could not carry our load because it was just too much for us. There was such restlessness; but when we came to the Lord, He gave us rest. This rest we have already received because He took our burdens away. Now, the Lord continues: "Take my yoke upon you and learn of me for I am meek and lowly in heart and ye shall find rest in your souls." Here are two kinds of rest. The first one is some-thing given. It is the rest in the spirit. The second is something that we must find which is the rest of the soul.

All who have come to the Lord Jesus have been given this rest in the spirit. We rest in the finished work of Christ. Our conscience enters into peace because the blood of the Lord Jesus has washed the conscience of our heart away from sins and accusations. However, after we have trusted the Lord and have been continuing on for a while, we discover our soul is restless. Our emotion is so in turmoil; our mind seems to be in constant battle and our will seems to be always changing direction. How can we find rest to our soul? The secret is: "Take my yoke upon you and learn of me." It is the yoke of our Lord. When He was on earth, He willingly and voluntarily put Himself under that yoke. Now a yoke is something put on the neck of the animal because without it no work could be done. The farmer could not plow the field if the animal wasn't under yoke. God can not do His work unless we are put under His yoke.

You know, lots of people try to serve God; but they do not want to be yoked. They want to be free and serve God in a free way. No one can do that! Even our Lord Jesus, when He came into this world to do the work of the Father, had to put His neck under the yoke. The yoke is something heavy which takes away your liberty and puts you under an obligation. You cannot do what you want because you are yoked. Our Lord Jesus took that voluntarily because of His love for the Father. "Not my will but Thine be done." Under that yoke He was able to complete the work of God.

The Lord said the reason you are restless is because you are too free. We think we are restless because we have no freedom; but it is just the contrary. We are restless because we are under no yoke. The Lord said: Take my yoke upon you. Be yoked together with Me. I am on one end; now put your neck under the other and learn of Me.

Even when we are put under the yoke, we still try to go our own way. We haven't learned; but just a look at the One with whom we are yoked and we begin to learn and know that He is strong enough not to let us pull Him off.

Dear brothers and sisters, if we want to have rest in our soul and rest in the Church corporately, then each of us must put ourselves under His yoke and learn of Him. There is much to be learned. Do not think that once you have chosen to put yourself under His yoke that you will take His will all the time. That is not so. Experience tells us that we need to be broken and it is very hard. Oh, how we need to look at the Lord, continuously learning of Him seeing His willingness, obedience and humbleness. Then, do you know what will happen? We find rest in our soul. Our heart will become meek and lowly as His. We will become selfless, flexible, pliable, humble and willing in the hand of God. The way to find rest in our soul is take the yoke and learn of the Lord.

As we set our heart toward the Lord we will not only have rest but there will be much building going on. You know, you cannot build when there is war. God did not allow David to build the temple because he was a man of war. A man of war can destroy but not build. You need a man of peace to build. We have a rest promised to us which is spoken of in the book of Hebrews—strive to enter into that rest which is to cease from our own work—and only as we enter into that rest will the building work begin. Oh, oftentimes we try to build and we find blood in our hands everywhere. We cannot build in that way. We have to be men of rest and peace before we can really build together. It is so important to have building going on among God's people.

The Lord said: "I will build my church upon this rock," and He will build it; but He will use us. He needs our cooperation. It is not just a matter of gathering stones and piling them one upon another. The stones must be fitted to each other. Then the house of God is built and when this happens, it is like fortified cities. The enemy will be defeated. Today the enemy is able to do so much havoc among God's people because we are not built together. There are no fortifications. If the enemy is able to scatter God's people, then he can deal with each one individually until everyone is finished. But, when God's people are built up together, it is like a fortification which can withstand all the assaults of the enemy. This happened under King Asa. Under that spiritual leadership the whole nation was encouraged to seek the Lord. They got rest and built cities and prospered before God. Now, may it be so with His people today!

After Asa built up an army and the fortified cities, strength was there. The enemy was aroused and he could not afford to be passive anymore. Everything that is of the Lord has to be tested; so after God prospered Asa in these ways, then came the test. Zerah the Ethiopian came out with a great army which was double that of King Asa's. They came with a host of a thousand thousand and three hundred chariots.

You know, dear brothers and sisters, there is a great difference between temptation and testing. Temptation comes from the enemy; testing comes from God. Temptation is trying to draw out the lust of the flesh in order to defeat us; but testing is drawing out the reserve which God has deposited in us that it may be further strengthened. Sometimes, however, we find when Satan tempts, God tests; but He will not allow us to be tempted beyond what we can bear. Why? Because when He allows Satan to tempt, He has already deposited enough in us to overcome that temptation. If this is not so, He will not allow that temptation to come to us. Brothers and sisters, this is our assurance. Oftentimes we think we are tempted beyond our measure. No such thing! If God allows the enemy to tempt us, He knows what He has already deposited in us and if we only look to Him, we will be able to overcome. Our reason for defeat is our not looking unto Him. We do not draw upon the resources which He has already deposited with-in.

By all appearances it seemed that the Ethiopians had much more than King Asa. But that is not so. Why? Because "little" with the Lord is much more than "many" without the Lord. Now hear what Asa says:

And Asa cried unto Jehovah his God, and said, Jehovah, it maketh no difference to thee to help, whether there be much or no power: help us, O Jehovah our God, for we rely on thee, and in thy name have we come against this multitude. Jehovah, thou art our God; let not man prevail against thee.

Oh, how we thank God for King Asa. He knew he could not meet the enemy; but, he knew he had a resource to rely upon. Notice that he said it made no difference whether there was much power or no power. Isn't that true? If God is for us, who can be against us?

Even if we have much power, we need God. That "much power" is still not enough and if we have "no power," that does not diminish anything because with God all things are possible. So, it is not in "much power" or "little power." It is in God! Oftentimes we find much power can be a hindrance because we will rely upon that instead of relying upon God and whenever you do that, you will find our power is not enough to meet the enemy. Sometimes it is better to have no power because knowing we are powerless causes us to depend on the Lord. You know, this is the reason we can overcome in big battles; but, in small ones we are overcome. The children of Israel could overcome Jericho but were defeated before Ai. This is very true in our lives because we think it depends upon much power or no power; but, it makes no difference because the power of God is made perfect in our weakness. Therefore, Paul said: "I boast of my weakness." Who will boast of his weakness? Either a fool or a man of God!

Here we see Asa committed the whole thing to the Lord saying: "Lord, it is your business. Do not let man prevail against Thee." If we commit ourselves to the Lord, He will commit Himself to us. The measure of our commitment to the Lord oftentimes governs the measure of His commitment to us. How much can you involve God? It depends upon how much you trust Him and how much

53

you have committed yourself to Him. If we wholeheartedly commit ourselves to Him, then we have involved Him and now it is no longer us. It is He! Let no man prevail against us. NO! Let no man prevail against THEE.

Oh, brothers and sisters, if we are brought to this point, how blessed it is to realize it is not our affair, our thing, our position, our power or glory; but it is the Lord's. The battle is the Lord's! When you are brought to this point based upon your full commitment to the Lord, you will hear Him say: "Yes, I will accept it. The battle is mine. I will fight for it."

Let's look at verse 12:

> And Jehovah smote the Ethiopians before Asa and before Judah; and the Ethiopians fled.

There was much victory and much spoil taken. We cannot avoid spiritual conflict. On the one hand as we follow the Lord wholly, there will be rest and building and on the other there will be conflict. There is bound to be spiritual conflict; but there is nothing to fear because every conflict is an opportunity to prove God. Each conflict will bring out the strength of God in us and also bring in much spoil for the Lord.

Humanly speaking it is quite difficult to combine these two things. How can we have conflict and rest at the same time? Spiritually this can be true. Sometimes they go on together. At other times there will be a period of rest and a period of conflict; but whatever it may be these are normal—very normal. Sometimes when God gives us a period of rest, we become complacent. We think all the problems are over; but, immediately there are problems, problems, problems. Thank God for that because He has to test us. He must test what He has done in us just like one who makes steel. After you have done so much to the iron, you must test it. This only brings out the strength.

When Asa came back with a victory, note how gracious God was. In chapter 15 we read:

> And the Spirit of God came upon Azariah the son of Oded. And he went out to meet Asa, and said to him, Hear ye me, Asa, and all Judah and Benjamin: Jehovah is with you while ye are with him; and if ye seek him he will be found of you, but if ye forsake him he will forsake you. (vv. 1-2)

Note the warning! Now verse 7: "But as for you, be firm and let not your hands be weak; for there is a reward for your deeds." This is almost a repeat of what happened in Genesis to Abraham. After he defeated the four kings and rescued his nephew Lot, he was coming back in victory and God sent Melchizedek, King of Salem, the High Priest of God, to meet him to remind him that it was the Lord who gave him the victory. He gave Abraham bread and wine to keep him in place before the Lord. Brothers and sisters, the greatest danger is after a great victory because there is often a let down. This can happen individually as well as corporately. After a great victory we tend to forget and think we have done it. Oh, how we need to be kept in place.

Asa was reminded by the prophet with these words: "The Lord is with you because you are with Him. If you seek Him, you will be rewarded. If you forsake Him, He will forsake you; but, be strong and seek Him for there is great reward for you." How we need such a warning because our heart is easily elated and uplifted and all so unconsciously! We have to be continually reminded that it is the Lord and not us. It has to be reaffirmed and reinforced.

Asa humbled himself before the Lord and listened to the words of the prophet. He took courage and put away all the abominations not only in the land of Judah but also Benjamin and even out of the cities which he had taken from Mount Ephraim and he renewed the altar of Jehovah that was before the porch of Jehovah. He assembled the people together and they made a covenant with God. How we thank God that he went from strength to strength. He made such a thorough work that he removed his mother from being queen mother because she made an idol. He destroyed the idol and removed it. He wanted to serve God wholly. Furthermore, he put into the house of God the things his father had dedicated and the things which he had dedicated—gold and silver and vessels. God gave him rest until the thirty-fifth year of his reign.

Here we can see that in seeking the Lord there is progress. In the beginning, because he sought the Lord, he removed all the abominations from the land of Judah and commanded the people to seek God. After the victory and the warning he even took courage and gathered up the abominations which were beyond his boundary. He made a covenant with God and dedicated things for God. In the temple of God there were gold and silver and vessels for the service of God. This is true. How can we enrich the service of the house of God? We can do so by dedicating gold and silver and vessels, not in the sense of material things since these things are none other than ourselves. We are vessels of honor. If we separate ourselves from the vessels of dishonor (that is, separating ourselves from the contentment of being vessels of dishonor) then we will be vessels of honor fit for the master's use in His house.

Now there was rest. So far so good! Under such leadership it was really good and the whole nation was benefited;

but, in the thirty-sixth year of his reign something happened. Now we know Asa had a heart for God; but, somehow his heart was not perfect. There was a flaw and it was found out in his later years. It is true when we get older that flaws, which seemed to be hidden during the younger years when we had more control of ourselves, begin to appear because we lose control of ourselves.

Baasha, king of Israel, came up against Judah and built Ramah in order to let none go out or come in to Asa, king of Judah. Because Asa became prosperous, being blessed by God, his influence extended over the boundary of his kingdom. People in the northern kingdom began to come over into Jerusalem to worship God and that, of course, created a problem.

King Baasha was frightened by all of this because the influence of King Asa penetrated into his kingdom. His people began to flock to the southern kingdom to worship God and if this continued, what would happen? Therefore, he rose up and built Ramah as a boundary in order to contain the influence of Asa. It was a "Berlin" wall! He built a "Berlin" wall trying to prevent his people from going to the south to worship God. He wanted to stop the good influence of King Asa. Now when Asa saw this, he became disturbed. Instead of seeking the Lord as he always did, he took gold and silver out of his own house and also the dedicated gold and silver in the house of God and gave them to Ben-hadad, King of Syria. He asked him to break his league with the king of Israel and to strengthen his league with him to attack Baasha, King of Israel. Well, he was successful in that strategy. Baasha left off building and Asa with his people took all the materials and built their own cities. Humanly speaking he was successful in doing that; but, notice these verses:

And at that time Hanani the seer came to Asa king of Judah, and said unto him, Because thou hast relied on the king of Syria, and hast not relied on Jehovah thy God, therefore has the army of the king of Syria escaped out of thy hand. Were not the Ethiopians and the Libyans a huge army, with very many chariots and horsemen? but when thou didst rely on Jehovah, he delivered them into thy hand. For the eyes of Jehovah run to and fro through the whole earth, to shew himself strong in the behalf or those whose heart is perfect toward him. Herein thou hast done foolishly; for from henceforth thou shalt have wars. (2 Chron.16:7-9)

Why did Asa who had begun and continued so well do such a foolish thing? Could it be, because he was so blessed by the Lord, that he became proud of himself and his strength? That is possible. Could it be that as the years went by his love for the Lord grew cold? That is also possible. Remember in Revelation chapter 2 the Lord's words to the church at Ephesus: "You have left your first love; therefore, I am against you." In the beginning he loved the Lord; but, now because he was so prosperous, he began to love himself more than the Lord. He loved the blessings of the Lord more than the Lord of blessing. Seeing his success he became so ambitious that he wanted his influence to overcome the whole nation of Israel; but, when he found his influence was contained, he was frightened. He wouldn't let it be so. Instead of inquiring of the Lord and relying upon Him as he did before with a much more difficult situation, he started to rely upon his own maneuvering. This was his first fault.

His second fault was the bribing of the king of Syria to break a league with the king of Israel. He did this with his money and the dedicated gold and silver in the temple.

What right did he have to rob God of the dedicated things? It showed how little respect he had for God. Isn't it strange that a leader who had begun and progressed so well with such blessings of the Lord could be so cold, self-centered and forgetful? How could he do such a thing even if it was successful? Oh, it would have been so much better if he had failed. Sometimes God gives in to our requests; but, He will send leanness to our soul.

When Asa was warned, instead of accepting it and humbling himself under the mighty hand of God, he was angry with the prophet and imprisoned him. From that time on his heart got harder and harder. He began to oppress some of his people. Think of that! What a warning to leadership. You know, the greatest temptation to leadership is success. If God does not give you success, you have no peril of this kind; but, if God gives you success, oh how easy it is for us to grow fat in our heart, becoming cold, ambitious and arrogant. Dear brothers and sisters, we see this even today. Many great leaders have fallen in their latter years because of success. We need to continually humble ourselves before the Lord.

In the thirty-ninth year of his reign a sad thing happened. Asa was diseased in his feet and could not walk. The disease was extremely great yet he did not seek Jehovah but the physicians. Even when he was disciplined by the Lord, instead of repenting, his heart was so hard that he did not even seek the Lord but only physicians. Is it because he thought he had failed God so much that he could not go to him and inquire? This is the deception of the enemy. Sometimes the enemy will deceive us and say: "You have gone too far and there is no more hope. What right do you have to go to the Lord and inquire of Him anymore?" But, no matter how low Asa fell he should have sought the Lord. Maybe the Lord would have healed him and maybe not; but, anyway he would have been restored. There was no restoration. He was hard to the very end! In the forty-first year of his reign after two years of his sickness he passed away.

The lesson here is in this word which we read in the beginning: "For the eyes of Jehovah run to and fro through the whole earth, to show himself strong in the behalf of those whose heart is perfect toward him." It is the picture not only of His looking around and looking back again; but also His looking deeper and deeper and deeper. Why does He look for a perfect heart? Because He wants to show His strength. There is no problem with the strength of God. The problem is the perfect heart. If there is a perfect heart, the strength of the Lord will be manifested. So we can see this matter of a perfect heart is very important.

What is a perfect heart? It is an undivided one. We cannot serve two masters. We cannot serve God and mammon. A divided heart will lead you no where. "Oh, unite my heart that I might serve Thee." A perfect heart is a pure one. There is no ulterior motive. You just want God to have everything. "Blessed are the pure in heart for they shall see God."

In the books of the Chronicles we see that God used David as a standard because he served God with a perfect heart; therefore, God measured every king according to David. David is not perfect; but, his heart is. You may find fault with his walk; but, his heart is perfect towards the Lord. Today God is looking for a perfect heart among His people especially with leadership. You don't need to be concerned as to whether or not God will show Himself strong in your behalf. Our concern should be: What about our heart? It is true our heart is deceitful above all things;

who can know it? We do not know our heart. It is God who tries our heart and ex-amines the reins. How important it is to pray like the psalmist:

> Search me, O God, and know my heart; prove me, and know my thoughts; And see if there be any grievous way in me; and lead me in the way everlasting. (Psalm 139:23-24)

We must lay our heart before the Lord asking Him to shine His light upon it to see if there is any flaw. If there is one, ask Him to remove it lest one day, because of that flaw, something will happen. It may not come out right now; but, one day it will.

We do thank God that He was not unmindful of King Asa even though his end was tragic. God gave him respect and honor from the people. When he was buried, they "laid him in a bed filled with spices, a mixture of divers kinds prepared by the perfumer's art; and they made a very great burning for him." God did not forget all the good he had done in his life; but, still, how much better it could have been if King Asa had served the Lord with a perfect heart. That would have given God more opportunity to show Himself strong. Oh, how God's strength is limited by us because our heart is imperfect. I do believe this is the central lesson which we have to learn and it is basic to leadership and, of course, to us all.

Our Heavenly Father, we do praise and thank Thee that Thy words are not just history; but Thy words are relevant to us today. They bring to us the eternal truth, the unchangeable principle of spiritual things. We do pray that we may learn these lessons from history. We ask Thee, O Lord, that Thou wilt be merciful to Thy people raising up spiritual leadership with a perfect heart towards Thee and we ask Thee to give Thy people a perfect heart that Thou mayest manifest Thyself and be strong in their behalf and it is all for Thy praise and glory. We ask in Thy precious name. Amen.

4—Spiritual Leadership—King Jehoshaphat

II Chronicles 20:20-27—And they rose early in the morning, and went forth towards the wilderness of Tekoa; and as they went forth, Jehoshaphat stood and said, Hear me, Judah, and ye inhabitants of Jerusalem! Believe in Jehovah your God, and ye shall be established; believe his prophets, and ye shall prosper! And he consulted with the people, and appointed singers to Jehovah, and those that should praise in holy splendour, as they went forth before the armed men, and say, Give thanks to Jehovah; for his loving- kindness endureth for ever! And when they began the song of triumph and praise, Jehovah set liers-in-wait against the children of Ammon, Moab, and mount Seir, who had come against Judah, and they were smitten. And the children of Ammon and Moab stood up against the inhabitants of mount Seir, to exterminate and destroy them; and when they had made an end of the inhabitants of Seir, they helped to destroy one another. And Judah came on to the mountain-watch in the wilderness, and they looked toward the multitude; and behold, they were dead bodies fallen to the earth, and none had escaped. And Jehoshaphat and his people came to plunder the spoil of them, and they found among them in abundance, both rices with the dead bodies, and precious things, and they stripped off themselves more than they could carry away; and they were three days in plundering the spoil, it was so much. And on the fourth day they assembled themselves in the valley of Berachah, for there they blessed Jehovah; therefore the name of that place was called The valley of Berachah, to this day.

We mentioned last night that in the books of the Chronicles we could see how important leadership is to a nation. When Judah had good kings who led the people back to God, then the whole nation was blessed, entered into rest and prospered by God. When there were bad kings who led the nation away from God, then the whole nation entered into ruin and curse. We know this is true even today. How important to have good spiritual leadership which will lead God's people into His full purpose. As you look around today seeing the conditions of the Church in general, I believe you will discover that this is a most vital and important thing. It doesn't mean that God's people are not responsible for what they are or do. Since we have the Holy Spirit in us, everyone is responsible and on the other hand leadership has much to do with the future of God's people. I believe there is much we can learn concerning leadership in the Chronicles. Of course, in a very general way it can be applied to everyone.

Last night we began with King Asa who had a marvelous beginning with God; but, towards the end he grew cold, became hard and even in the very last days he did not seek the Lord but only the physicians. I hope we learned some lessons. This evening we would like to go to another good king—Jehoshaphat. When he came to the throne he was thirty-five years old and his father Asa had been on the throne for forty-one years. By this we can see that Jehoshaphat was born in the early days of the reign of King Asa, that is during the times when he did what was right and good in the sight of God serving Him faithfully. Notice that this young man Jehoshaphat, instead of following in the fallen footsteps of his father Asa during those last years, learned the good lessons he should have. His father's hardness of heart served as a warning to him and he was encouraged to serve God with a perfect heart. When we see something before us, there is the possibility of two kinds of reaction: One will be following the bad example. The other, seeing how bad it is, will be that by the grace of God we let it push us even more to the Lord. How we hope this will be the way in which we learn. Whenever we see something that could be a warning, we should take it to heart that we might double our efforts in trying to follow the Lord.

So Jehoshaphat not only did not walk in the ways of his father Asa in the latter days but he walked according to the early ways of his father David. Throughout the books of the Chronicles God always uses David as the standard. He measures every leadership with David. Just to follow Asa is not enough, even to walk in the early days of Asa is not enough. You have to go back to the early days of his father David.

Now, what is meant by "the early ways of his father David?" This will bring us back to the time of David when he was a shepherd watching a few sheep in the wilderness. He was unknown by men, neglected by his father and despised by his brothers. During those days he developed a heart for God and learned to trust in the Lord. When the lion and bear came out, David in the power of God, destroyed them and rescued the sheep. God delivered him from the paws of the lion and the bear. These are David's first ways. You remember after he was manifested to the children of Israel, he was persecuted by King Saul and for ten years had to flee as a fugitive hiding in caves and strongholds. Yet, during those days in spite of all the adversities, it drove him closer to God. He was so obedient to God that he did not even lift his hand against his enemy Saul when God seemed to deliver him into his hands. David not only had a perfect heart but perfect ways.

As we look further into the life of David after he became king, we know something happened. Even though his heart was still perfect towards the Lord, his ways were no longer perfect in the matter of Uriah's wife and the matter of counting the people of Israel. So you will find that even though his heart was still perfect, his ways were not as perfect but looking into the early ways of David they were perfect and these are the ways in which Jehoshaphat walked.

Dear brothers and sisters, what is God looking for in leadership and His people in general? First, it is a perfect heart. It is more important than anything else. You must have a heart that is utterly towards God. Second, it is your ways. You may have a perfect heart towards God; but, how about your ways? Are you really walking in humble obedience to the Lord in all of your ways? It does not satisfy God's heart if you are just a little better than someone else. Oftentimes we compare ourselves with others, even with the former generation thinking we are better than they; but, that is not enough because the only standard which God sets up for us is Christ. He is the Golden Rod—the only measurement which God has. He will measure every heart and every way with Christ.

Look at Christ! How meek and lowly is His heart! Look at His ways! He was obedient to the Father even unto death and the death of the cross. This is what God expects of us because we have the life of Christ in us; therefore, He will not accept anything else. Only the standard of Christ satisfies God.

Since Jehoshaphat began in such a way, it is no wonder that God prospered him. He had honor and riches in abundance. Today, of course, in the new covenant we are not expecting honor and riches in a material way. It may not work that way; but, it does work spiritually because God has blessed us with every spiritual blessing in the heavenlies in Christ Jesus. If we serve the Lord with a perfect heart and walk in all the ways of Christ, surely God will bless us.

In the third year of Jehoshaphat's reign he sent out his princes and priests to teach the people. They traveled throughout the nation to the cities of Judah teaching the people to fear the Lord. For the building of God's house there is a place for teaching. Whenever there is a real heart towards the Lord and a walk according to the Lord, there will be a teaching ministry going to the people because that ministry comes out of your own walk and experience with the Lord. This will build the nation and strengthen God's people in a very marvelous way.

After God gave Jehoshaphat honor and riches in abundance, he would not walk in the ways of Israel because Ahab was king at that time and he was very wicked. He led the whole nation away from Jehovah God to worship Baals. Jehoshaphat separated himself completely from Israel because it was a bad example; but, there is something we cannot understand. Jehoshaphat allied himself with Ahab by marriage. It is hard to understand how a person, who saw so clearly this bad influence of Israel, could do such a thing. We can't explain it. Now there is a flaw in his walk. Instead of being separated he joined himself to King Ahab by the most intimate union— marriage. Why? Is it because Ahab, seeing the prosperity of Jehoshaphat, tried to get his help by laying a trap? That is possible. Or was it because Jehoshaphat in his great zeal for the Lord hoped the nations of Israel and Judah would be rejoined and took the way of expediency? This, too, was possible.

Dear brothers and sisters, wherever there is separation the enemy will try everything to break it down because he knows separation is power. This could be a reason for Ahab's trying to lay a trap and innocently catching Jehoshaphat.

Let us look at unity and see that it never comes by compromise. In the prayer of our Lord Jesus in John 17 we see the main burden of our Lord is that we may be one as He and the Father are one. He not only prayed this for His immediate disciples but for those who would believe in Him through them. In other words He had the whole Church in view. This was the burning desire of the Lord; but, before He asked the Father this, He said they are not of this world as I am not of this world. So you cannot have oneness in Christ unless there is separation from the world. The reason for God's people not being one today is because there is too much of the world in us. If it is Christ, we are not divided. We cannot be. Is Christ divided? It is the world in us that hinders our oneness. Separation is the step to oneness. This principle is often overlooked. People often try to maintain oneness by compromise and I wonder if that is what Jehoshaphat did. He adopted the way of expediency and sacrificed principle which he had kept very faithfully. This does not work. On the contrary the evil always has the upper hand. Instead of helping Ahab and the nation of Israel back to God Ahab drew Jehoshaphat into helping him and he nearly lost his life.

The teaching of the word is, "Be not unequally yoked with unbelievers" because there is nothing in common. If we separate, then the Lord says: "...and I will receive you; and I will be to you for a Father, and ye shall be to me for sons and daughters, saith the Lord Almighty." El Shaddai, the All Sufficient God!

Therefore we must purify ourselves from the pollution of the flesh and of the spirit as we read in 2 Corinthians chapter 7. This is a lesson which we have to take to heart. Unfortunately many of God's people despise the plain word of God. The word of God says, "Be ye not unequally yoked..." In Deuteronomy chapter 22 it is forbidden to plow with an ass and an ox because they have different temperaments. They are entirely different. There is no fellowship between light and darkness, between Christ and Belial, between righteousness and lawlessness, believers and unbelievers, the temple of God and idols. They have nothing in common. "Be ye not unequally yoked..."

Unfortunately Jehoshaphat deviated somehow from the early ways of his father David. He allied himself with Ahab by marriage and once that ally was founded, he couldn't break it. This thing followed him throughout his life and even after he died. He made an unholy ally with King Ahab when his son Jehoram married the daughter of Ahab, Athaliah.

After a certain time Jehoshaphat went to visit Ahab. Ahab killed many sheep and oxen to entertain him; but, he did not do this just for the sake of entertainment. He had an ulterior motive. He asked him to go with him to fight against Ramoth-Gilead. This was a city of refuge. According to the book of Joshua, after the children of Israel entered into the promised land, God asked them to set apart cities as places of refuge where people could flee and have their life preserved when they did anything innocently. Probably Ahab used this as a pretext. Here was a city of refuge

69

supposed to be used by God and now it was in the hands of the Syrians. Certainly we should get it back for God. Jehoshaphat said: "I am as thou and my people as thou. I will be with thee in the war." Because of the unholy alliance Jehoshaphat could not get away. He joined himself to Ahab and now he had to serve Ahab's purpose.

We do know that Jehoshaphat had some kind of uneasy feeling in him. He knew he was not quite right; therefore, he asked if they could inquire of the prophet first. Of course, he should have done this before he gave the promise; so as he drew back a little, he decided to inquire of the prophet.

Ahab had many prophets—400 of them who were prophets of Baal. He gathered all these together and, of course, being false prophets they would prophesy what Ahab would like for them to say. They all said to go ahead and God would deliver the enemy into their hands; but, Jehoshaphat knew better and said: "Is there a prophet of the Lord here?" Ahab answered: "Yes, there is one; but, he never says anything good about me." This reminds me of a story. In the old days a missionary went to Africa and gave the chief a mirror. When the chief looked into the mirror, he smashed it to pieces because he saw that ugly figure. So Ahab, instead of seeing himself in the light of God, hated God's light.

The prophet Micah son of Imlah was called and he was even warned by the messenger that every prophet was saying some-thing good so why don't you follow suit. Micah replied that whatever God said that would be what he would declare.

In the beginning of the conversation when King Ahab asked whether they should go or not, they had already decided to go. So Micah without inquiring of the Lord said:

"Go ye up and prosper; and they will be given into your hands." Ahab knew he was just teasing him and not telling the truth. He said: "How many times shall I adjure thee that thou tell me nothing but truth in the name of Jehovah?" Micah replied: "I saw all Israel scattered upon the mountains, as sheep that have no shepherd...let them return every man to his house in peace." "And the king of Israel said to Jehoshaphat, Did I not tell thee that he prophesies no good concerning me, but evil?"

Unfortunately, in spite of the warning of the prophet, Jehoshaphat was so involved that he still went to war with Ahab. Think of that! Now Ahab had some premonition and he was a little bit afraid. He said to Jehoshaphat: "I will disguise myself, and will enter into the battle; but put thou on thy robes." He was tricking Jehoshaphat and Jehoshaphat was so innocent that he fell for it. All the captains of the Syrians surrounded Jehoshaphat because they were supposed to fight only the king of Israel. Jehoshaphat cried out and God heard him and diverted the captains from him. If it had not been for the Lord, Jehoshaphat could have died on the battlefield.

Oh, brothers and sisters, how often we think so lightly of God's word. Even knowing God's word, "Be ye not unequally yoked with unbelievers," we still try it. We think perhaps it won't be that serious. Isn't that like the serpent? We so often fall in this respect. We can die. If there had not been the mercy of the Lord, Jehoshaphat would have died. He would have died for Ahab. Apply this to anything in our Christian life and you will find the same truth. It is only the mercy of the Lord that keeps us alive.

Then we read that someone just shot an arrow aimlessly and it hit Ahab and he died. What a lesson to us! How we need to be in fear and trembling before the Lord.

In 2 Corinthians 5 Paul mentions two things: (1) Knowing the terror of the Lord; (2) Being constrained by the love of Christ. I believe these two go together. We often emphasize the love of Christ. "For the love of Christ constrains us, having judged this: that one died for all, then all have died; and he died for all, that they who live should no longer live to themselves, but to him who died for them and has been raised." This is true. But oftentimes we forget the other side—the terror of the Lord. Our Lord is a consuming fire. We need to know the terribleness of the Lord and if we do, we dare not tempt Him. Oh, sometimes we take the love of Christ and overstretch it in such a way that we think we can do anything and get by with it. There is not a holy fear in us. Love and holy fear go together.

Now it is true in 1 John it says: "...perfect love casts out fear..." The reason we are afraid is because love is not perfect; but, here the fear is one of a different kind. It is the fear of punishment. If there is perfect love, you will not fear the punishment. Of course, this does not mean that in perfect love there is not that element of fear lest we displease Him. That kind of fear is always present with love. You want to always please Him; so, Paul said: "Whether I live or die my ambition is to please the Lord, knowing the terror of the Lord." We must learn this.

During our time there has been a reaction and I believe it has gone a little too far. Well, maybe today it is becoming more balanced. You know, five or ten years ago there was a reaction among God's people, especially the young, that everything is just "love." There was no reverence or fear. Now maybe the former generation overdid it in the other direction. They seemed to have reverence yet were in bondage; therefore, the pendulum swung to the other side and you think of nothing but love. Everything is love and because it is love everything is all right. There is no reverence of fear whatsoever. What a mess! There must be the love of Christ and the terror of the Lord.

Jehoshaphat did come back in peace and it was because of the mercy of the Lord. You know, sometimes there are unholy alliances; but, through the mercy of the Lord God intervenes and rescues; however, this is no excuse for us to neglect God's word. It is the mercy of the Lord.

We read that God sent a prophet to Jehoshaphat, Jehu the son of Hanani. Remember when King Asa trusted in his own diplomacy instead of trusting in the power of God. He was successful; but, when he came back, God sent Hanani the prophet to tell him that he had done foolishly and he would not listen. He rebelled against the discipline of the Lord. Jehoshaphat his son also did something foolish and nearly lost his life; so, God sent Jehu the son of Hanani to him saying:

> Shouldest thou help the ungodly, and love them that hate Jehovah? Therefore is wrath upon thee from Jehovah. Nevertheless there are good things found in thee; for thou hast put away the Asherahs out of the land, and hast directed thy heart to seek God. (II Chronicles 19:2-3)

Jehu strongly reprimanded him telling him he was now under God's discipline. How did Jehoshaphat react to this discipline? It was very different from that of his father Asa who acted violently putting the prophet into prison and oppressing some of his people. His heart was hardened. Thank God Jehoshaphat, when God's discipline came upon him, bowed himself under the mighty hand of God. Dear brothers and sisters, whenever we are under God's discipline, we can resist and be hardened or we can bow under His hand and in due time He will exalt us.

Jehoshaphat accepted the discipline and even encouraged himself to serve God in a perfect way. He again traveled throughout his country and brought them back to Jehovah the God of their fathers. He set up judges and admonished them to judge righteously. In other words he not only desired that he serve God with a perfect heart; but, he also desired the whole nation to serve with him. This is the result of discipline.

I often think this: God does not punish us; He disciplines us. To people who do not know God they are punished; but, for us who are the Lord's we are disciplined by God in order to be restored to Him. If we yield ourselves under His discipline, even out of weakness and failure, there will be increase and that is the grace of God.

Because Jehoshaphat yielded himself under the disciplinary hand of the Lord, God began to exalt and increase him. The enemy couldn't stand this and we read in chapter 20, verse 1: "And it came to pass after this that the children of Moab, and the children of Ammon, and with them certain of the Maonites, came against Jehoshaphat to battle." Great multitudes came, the Moabites, the Ammonites and the Maonites, all joining together to fight against Jehoshaphat. Whenever God's people really set their hearts towards Him to serve Him and there is increase, you find the enemy will come and immediately there will be spiritual conflict.

When the great multitude came, what did Jehoshaphat do? "And Jehoshaphat feared, and set himself to seek Jehovah, and proclaimed a fast throughout Judah" (2 Chronicles 20:3). He knew there was no strength in himself; but, he set his face to seek the Lord. He proclaimed a fast and all the people gathered together in a great congregation not only the men but also the women and their little ones and their sons. Jehoshaphat prayed and reminded God of His promise: "If evil come upon us, sword, judgment, or pestilence, or famine, and we stand before this house and before thee—for thy name is in this house—and cry unto thee in our distress, then thou wilt hear and save" (II Chronicles 20:9). Jehoshaphat laid hold of the promise of God and also reminded Him that when the children of Israel came to the promised land, God did not allow them to take the land of Moab, Ammon and Mt. Seir. Now these people were coming to take their land from them. In other words he reminded God of His righteousness. God is righteous. He told the Lord, "...our eyes are upon thee" (v.12). He transferred the whole matter to God.

Dear brothers and sisters, I believe this is what we find in Philippians. "Rejoice in the Lord always: ... Be careful about nothing; but in everything, by prayer and supplication with thanksgiving, let your requests be made known to God ..." (Philippians 4:4, 6). You learn to transfer everything to God. We cannot expect there will be no war, no conflict, no problem. If we know how to transfer everything to God and say: "Now, Lord, it is Your business; not ours," the result will be God will take it up. He will say: "The battle is Mine. You don't need to fight. I am going to fight because it is my business."

The Lord told the people to go out and watch and He would do the work. When the word of God came in that way, Jehoshaphat had perfect faith in the Lord and he and the people bowed down and worshiped and praised God.

The next morning when Jehoshaphat consulted with the people, he "appointed singers to Jehovah, and those that should praise in holy splendour, as they went forth before the armed men, and say, Give thanks to Jehovah; for his loving-kindness endureth for ever!" When they began to sing praises, God began to work. We usually sing praises after the work is done; but, here they sing before the work is done. They believed as though it were already done and this is faith. This reminds us of Mark chapter 11 when the Lord Jesus cursed the fig tree and it withered. The next day Peter pointed it out to the Lord and said: "...see, the fig tree which thou cursedst is dried up." The Lord answered: "Have faith in God." Literally it is, "Have the faith of God." What kind of faith does God have? This kind:

> Verily I say to you, that whosoever shall say to this mountain, Be thou taken away and cast into the sea, and shall not doubt in his heart, but believe that what he says takes place, whatever he shall say shall come to pass for him. For this reason I say to you, All things whatsoever ye pray for and ask, believe that ye receive it, and it shall come to pass for you. (Mark 11:23-24)

In other words you receive it in faith first and then you will receive it in fact. Faith comes before fact! Because you have the faith of God you can praise Him first as if it is already done.

Faith is a very important element in leadership. You cannot lead if you don't have faith in God. You need the faith of God in order to lead the people into victory. Everyone can praise if they want after the work is done; but, not many people can praise before they see it in fact. It is only those who have the eyes of faith that can do this.

Of course, you cannot create faith; you have to see God. If you see God, then faith is given. Even though the fact has not yet come, to the eyes of faith God has already done it. I remember Brother Nee used to say: "What is faith? Not only God is able and not only God is willing; but, God has done it. That is faith." You know, praise is not to be used as a formula to induce God. That will not work. Praise has to be in faith. Then you find it works because you have already seen it.

After that great victory, they gathered spoil for three days. How often we gather the spoil and return home and just try to enjoy ourselves; but, this was not so with Jehoshaphat. On the fourth day he led the people into the valley of Berachah and praised the Lord. In other words they humbled themselves before the Lord and praised Him knowing that everything comes from God. Now, that is important! So, we do thank God for this man Jehoshaphat.

Before we close there is another warning. Remember the unholy alliance Jehoshaphat had with King Ahab. Even after Ahab's death the influence of that was still touching Jehoshaphat's life. Ahab's son, Ahaziah who did wickedly, joined with Jehoshaphat to build ships desiring to go to Tarshish for wealth—a joint business enterprise. God was not pleased with that and broke the ships. Also if you read 1 Kings chapter 22 you will see Jehoshaphat was asked to do the same thing again; but, he would not because he had learned his lesson.

This is still not the end. After Jehoshaphat died and also his son Jehoram, notice what happened. Athaliah, daughter of Ahab, came and seized the nation of Judah and reigned over that nation for a period. One step in the wrong direction and the result continues on. I believe this is a real warning to us today. How we need to walk carefully before the Lord not only maintaining a perfect heart towards Him; but, walk in the ways of the Lord—every step. If you miss a step, you never know what the result will be. It can continue on.

You can find this in the life of David. Wars never left his household. They continued on even after he died. How important this is. This shows us how fallible we are. Never think because you are blessed of the Lord you become infallible. Also this is no excuse for us to fall. This should be a warning to us that we may walk all our lives softly before the Lord.

Our Heavenly Father, we do praise and thank Thee that Thou dost not hide anything from us. Thou dost show us how we should walk rightly before Thee and Thou dost show us how possible it is for us to go astray and how serious it can be. So, Lord, we ask Thee that all these lessons may be taken to heart. Oh, we pray that Thou wilt keep us always in the spirit of humility walking softly before Thee and serving Thee with a perfect heart. Oh, that Thy people may be blessed. In the Name of our Lord Jesus. Amen.

5—Right Leadership—King Hezekiah

II Chronicles 29:1-11—Hezekiah began to reign being twenty-five years old; and he reigned twenty-nine years in Jerusalem; and his mother's name was Abijah, daughter of Zechariah. And he did what was right in the sight of Jehovah, according to all that David his father had done.

He, in the first year of his reign, in the first month, opened the doors of the house of Jehovah, and repaired them. And he brought in the priests and the Levites, and gathered them into the open place eastward; and he said to them, Hear me, ye Levites: hallow yourselves now, and hallow the house of Jehovah the God of your fathers, and carry forth the filthiness out of the sanctuary. For our fathers have transgressed, and done evil in the sight of Jehovah our God, and have forsaken him and turned away their faces from the habitation of Jehovah, and have turned their backs. Also they have shut up the doors of the porch, and put out the lamps, and have not burned incense nor offered up burnt-offerings in the sanctuary to the God of Israel. Therefore the wrath of Jehovah has been upon Judah and Jerusalem, and he has delivered them to vexation, to desolation, and to hissing, as ye see with your eyes. And behold, our fathers have fallen by the sword, and our sons and our daughters and our wives are in captivity for this. Now it is in my heart to make a covenant with Jehovah the God of Israel, that his fierce anger may turn away from us. My sons, be not now negligent; for Jehovah has chosen you to stand before him, to do service unto him, and to be his ministers and incense- burners.

II Chronicles 29:36—And Hezekiah rejoiced, and all the people, that God had prepared the people; for the thing was done suddenly.

II Chronicles 31:20-21—And thus did Hezekiah throughout Judah, and wrought what was good and right and true before Jehovah his God. And in every work that he undertook in the service of the house of God, and in the law, and in the commandments, to seek his God, he did it with all his heart and prospered.

II Chronicles 32:20, 22-26—And because of this, king Hezekiah and the prophet Isaiah the son of Amoz prayed and cried to heaven.

In those days Hezekiah was sick unto death, and he prayed to Jehovah; and he spoke to him and gave him a sign. But Hezekiah rendered not again according to the benefit done to him, for his heart was lifted up; and there was wrath upon him, and upon Judah Jerusalem. And Hezekiah humbled himself for the pride of his heart, he and the inhabitants of Jerusalem, so that the wrath of Jehovah came not upon them in the days of Hezekiah.

Last time when we were together, we mentioned two of the kings of Judah, Asa and Jehoshaphat. God willing, we would like to continue on and the king we will focus upon will be Hezekiah. We are told, according to Jewish estimate, there were three kings who were quite superior. One, of course, was David and another was Hezekiah. He was among the three kings who were the most honored by the Jewish nation. As we look into his background, we find he had the worst father a son could ever have. His father Ahaz was a very wicked king.

In chapter 28, verse 22 we read: "And in the time of his trouble he transgressed yet more against Jehovah, this king Ahaz." Because of the hardness of his heart towards the Lord, he and his nation were brought into humiliation; but, when he was in trouble, instead of humbling himself asking for forgiveness and turning to the Lord, he transgressed more against Jehovah. "This king Ahaz"—this is the comment of the Holy Spirit. Yet out of such a wicked father came forth one of the best kings of the nation of Judah. We wonder how this can be. The only explanation is the sovereign mercy of God. Because of His love towards his people God gave them one of the best kings so that the lamp of the house of David might not be quickly extinguished.

When you read the Scripture, sometimes you think there are things which are insignificant. For instance a number of times in the Kings and Chronicles you find the mother of the king is mentioned. This we find in chapter 29, verse 1: "...and his mother's name was Abijah, daughter of Zechariah." Why is her name mentioned? Of course, the influence of a father upon a child is great; but, the influence of a mother is equally significant. Hezekiah had a very bad father, ungodly, wicked; but, probably he had a very good mother. We believe this is why her name is mentioned. Perhaps when he was a child, she brought him up in the fear of the Lord and in spite of everything his father did, he did not depart from the way he was taught as a child.

It is so important for sisters to realize this. It is true that when a child is growing and in his teens, he will follow more of his father's ways looking up to him; but, when he is very young being more under the care of his mother he will look up more to her. Therefore if a child is being instructed in the fear of the Lord in the early days of his life, even his father cannot change him. So I want to encourage mothers that as God entrusts children to you, this is your opportunity. Do not wait until your children grow up and are then maybe under some bad influence. I do hope you fathers are a good influence also. In the early years which are the important formative ones, that is the time when the mother's responsibility is great.

When Hezekiah was twenty-five years old, he ascended to the throne. He was completely different from his father because he did what was right in the sight of the Lord ac-cording to all that David his father had done. Remember, God measures every king with David. He was God's yardstick for kingship because he was a king after God's own heart. David's heart, action and deeds were the yardstick which God used to measure every king in the nation of Judah. If you read very carefully, you find some of the kings failed completely because they did not walk in the ways of their father David. They followed in the ways of the kings of Israel or sometimes even the nations. They completely failed God. There were others who did some of the things which David did; but, their heart was not perfect towards God as his was. Then there are a few, and Hezekiah was one of them, whose heart was perfect towards God and who did everything right in the sight of God as David had done.

Today, dear brothers and sisters, we are kings and priest unto God. He has a golden measuring rod with which to measure all our deeds, thoughts and even our hearts. He measures us with Christ. God gives no other standard but His own Son. Even though He knows our frailty and frame, He will not lower His standard. He has given His Son to us and He is in us. Knowing this is the measurement which God uses, how we need to humble ourselves before the Lord continuously. There is no place for you to be proud. In the things we do, since we are measured by Christ, how often we fall short of the glory of God; but, as we recognize our weaknesses, then His strength is made perfect in us. In other words we realize God has no other standard than Christ. One day in the New Jerusalem everything will be measured by that golden rod—the standard of Christ. At that time we will arrive at the fullness of the stature of Christ. This, however, must begin today while we are still on earth.

Hezekiah did everything right in the sight of God as David had done. As soon as he ascended the throne, in the first year of the first month, he started his work of restoration. His father had broken all the vessels in the house of God, closed the door of the temple and erected many idols; so, the first thing Hezekiah did was call the Levites and priests together encouraging and exhorting them to sanctify themselves and the temple. Within sixteen days the temple was cleansed and the altar was cleansed and ready to receive sacrifices. This was a very speedy restoration. It was because Hezekiah's heart was perfect towards God and also the people had prepared hearts.

There are two things here which should be lessons to us. One is the matter of leadership. It is so important that there be good leadership among God's people. You know, God's people, as the Bible says, are the flock, the sheep of God's pasture. On one hand sheep are very innocent and on the other they are the most ignorant. When a sheep gets into thorns or thistles, it doesn't know how to extricate itself. Until it is delivered, it has to remain there. If a sheep gets lost, it can never find its way home. I think this is a perfect description of God's people—so innocent, yet at times so ignorant and easily led astray. As you see the situation of God's people over the world today, you do not have the heart to blame them because they are so innocent. God's people are good—they love the Lord, have a heart for Him; yet so many of them are led astray into all kinds of things, some unthinkable.

Because God's people are like this, leadership is so important. In Ephesians chapter 4 there are four classes of people whom God has given as His gifts to the Church, "...some apostles, and some prophets, and some evangelists, and some shepherds and teachers..." All those whom God raises up as leaders in the Church are under-shepherds. They should walk before the flock finding pasture knowing the difference between poisonous herbs and good grass. They should protect the flock from harm and find the still waters for them. They should be examples to the sheep.

What a tragedy if the leadership is wrong because the sheep will just follow the shepherd into death. If the leadership is right, great blessings will be upon God's people; so, we must look to the Lord asking that He raise up right leadership like King Hezekiah. Because of the right leadership under Hezekiah the whole situation changed within a month. Through the years Ahaz caused much evil drawing the nation into idolatry, rebellion and wickedness; but, within a month the entire situation could be changed because of right leadership.

Yes, the right leadership can change things very quickly; but, there is also the responsibility of the people. Hezekiah had a heart for the Lord and desired to lead the people back to God; but, without a prepared people and the cooperation of the priests and Levites, there was not much he could do by himself. We need leadership and we need a prepared people. These two must work together or God's work will be delayed.

Within sixteen days everything was ready—the temple was cleansed; the door was opened; the priests and Levites were ready to serve and sacrifices were ready to be offered to the Lord. The first thing to do was offer sin offerings and burnt offerings. As you read, you find these were not just offered for the King nor just for the nation of Judah but for all of Israel. Remember, at the time of Hezekiah the Northern Kingdom of Israel was already destroyed—ten tribes were taken into Assyrian captivity. After the offerings were restored, Hezekiah sent messengers into the northern cities which were not under his control. The restoration in the nation of Judah spread even to the other cities. These messengers were sent from Beer-sheba to Dan through the country of Ephraim and Manasseh, even to Zebulun to call them to come and keep the Passover with them. Now when this was done, the messengers were ridiculed by those people. Think of that! Those people in the Northern Kingdom had already seen the judgment of God upon them; yet, when they were called to come to Jerusalem to keep the Passover, they ridiculed the messengers. Their heart was so hardened. Thank God, there were still some from Asher, Manasseh and Zebulun that responded and came to Jerusalem to keep the Passover.

Now it is true the Passover was not kept at the usual time which should be the fourteenth day of the first month; but, the people were not ready. Therefore it was kept in the second month which was irregular. Furthermore the people that came from the north ate the Passover without being cleansed. They were not prepared and this was sinful against God; but, Hezekiah prayed and God forgave them. After they kept the Passover for seven days, they decided, since it was so good, they would like to keep another seven days. Again this was unusual; but, from it you find everything was restored. The Passover was the foundation to the history of the nation of Israel. It was by the Passover that they were delivered and brought to Mount Sinai and became a nation unto God. Everything went back to the very foundation. The foundation was strengthened and on that everything was built according to God's original purpose. Again and again you see in the descriptions that everything was done according to the law of Moses, according to David, according to Nathan, according to the prophets. Everything was restored to the original design and purpose. Now that was a recovery—full and complete!

As you read on, you find not only the Passover was kept; but, the courses of the priests were restored and all their needs were abundantly supplied. People brought in their tithes and first-fruits and it was over-abundant. Everything spoke of the abundance of the Lord. What a testimony! In chapter 31 we read:

And thus did Hezekiah throughout Judah, and wrought what was good and right and true before Jehovah his God. And in every work that he undertook in the service of the house of God, and in the law, and in the commandments, to seek his God, he did it with all his heart and prospered.(vv.20-21)

Here you find this matter of restoration. What must be recovered? The house of God must be recovered and it must be cleansed. The priests, the Levitical service, must be recovered. The sacrifices and feasts must be recovered and the supplies in the house of God. Apply this to our time. If God would raise up the right leadership and prepare His people, there will be restoration and recovery. The first thing to be recovered, of course, is the house of God. Every sin will be purged. There will be repentance. There will be humbling before God. If God's people will humble themselves and pray, then God will build them up together as a habitation of God in the spirit.

When our Lord Jesus was on earth, He, at the beginning and end of His public ministry, entered the temple in Jerusalem and cleansed it. These two times sum up His feeling towards the house of God.

> ... and said to the sellers of doves, Take these things hence; make not my Father's house a house of merchandise. (John 2:16)

> And he says to them, It is written, My house shall be called a house of prayer, but ye have made it a den of robbers. (Matthew 21:13)

Our Lord's heart is always upon the house because it is the purpose of God to dwell among His people and this, dear brothers and sisters, has not changed. How He loves to dwell at peace and rest in that house.

Today the house is no longer a physical one. It is spiritual. It is built with living stones such as we are; but, much cleansing is needed. Sometimes you feel the door to the house is almost closed. When people really desire to worship the Lord, where can they go? Where can they find the Lord among His people? If we really want the presence of the Lord and truly desire to see His glory, then there is nothing more important than His glory fill the house. What is a house if there is no glory? It is empty! For the glory to fill His house there must be much cleansing and much humbling before the Lord.

In I Peter 2:5 we read: "...yourselves also, as living stones, are being built up a spiritual house, a holy priesthood, to offer spiritual sacrifices acceptable to God by Jesus Christ." Not only are we to be built up together in such a way that the glory of the Lord may be manifested, but we are a holy priesthood. Holy means "set apart." We are "other worldly," not belonging to this world—uncommon—a holy priesthood. How we need to be sanctified, set apart, that we may serve together.

In the case of Hezekiah the Levites sanctified themselves even more diligently than the priests. They really put the priests to shame. Today it should not be just a few priests serving but a priesthood—all of God's people. There is a service for everyone and we serve coordinately under our High Priest, the Lord Jesus Christ who is now represented by the Holy Spirit. When the Holy Spirit is leading His people in that priestly service, whether it is in the time of worship, prayer or sharing, there are no jarring notes, disjointed things or distractions.

Then there are the sacrifices. All the sacrifices in the Scripture, whether sin offering, burnt offering, trespass offering, peace offering or meal offering, are the various expressions of Christ. Of course, you know we offer spiritual sacrifices and as we together are a priesthood, we offer back to God the Christ that He has revealed to us. When this happens, what riches we will experience in the house of God. Everything is abundantly supplied with no lack. Don't forget, this is not just for the nation of Judah; it is for all Israel. It will overflow. We can never be exclusive. We must not think just of ourselves—that if God is with us, we don't care if He is with His other children. Brothers and sisters, no! We are one body; we are one nation. In the recovery work of Hezekiah, even though many did reject it, it had to spread to all Israel. Some would be touched and drawn into this worship, praise and recovery.

So we do believe that in our day the same thing can happen. How we need to look to the Lord that He might give us the right leadership and a prepared people. Everyone of us is responsible. We cannot look to those in responsibility and put the blame on them. It is true they have to bear that responsibility; but we need to look within ourselves and see how much we are prepared, how much we cooperate and how much we support the leadership, working together for the glory of the Lord.

In chapter 32, verse 1 we read: "After these things and this faithfulness, Sennacherib king of Assyria came and entered into Judah, and encamped against the fortified cities, and thought to break into them." Whenever there is something recovered to the original design, it will be severely tested. Spiritual conflict comes immediately. "After these things and this faithfulness ..." Do not think that if we are faithful, we have smooth sailing. No! If we are faithful, then the enemy will be aroused. The Lord said, "I will build my church upon this rock" and immediately He said, "and the gates of Hades shall not prevail against it."

The Lord has not promised that the gates of Hades will not be opened or that there will be no attack; but, He has promised that the gates of Hades shall not prevail against it.

King Sennacherib of Assyria came with this army into the land of Judah with the intention of destroying it just as he had destroyed the nation of Israel. By all human computation and outward appearances this would be the case. At that time no nation could stand against the King of Assyria. Assyria had destroyed many nations. It was not a matter of boasting when the King of Assyria said, "Which God or which nation could deliver them from my hands?" He did destroy many nations but their god was no god.

Hezekiah realized he had no power to stand against Sennacherib so he tried to do his best by redirecting the water so that it could be directed into the city that the enemy might not have it. He tried to build the walls as high as the tower. He tried everything he could think of and he should have; but, in spite of all this which he had done, he knew it was no match for Sennacherib. He did what he should have and then he trusted the Lord. We will not go into the details; but, if you want to know them, they are found in 2 Kings and Isaiah. Chronicles does not give us the historical details; but, they do give us the spiritual history.

Sennacherib sent his general to Jerusalem to lay siege upon it. How he blasphemed the name of the Lord as if God was like the other gods who were no gods at all. Hezekiah asked the people not to answer; but, he and Isaiah went to the Lord and prayed. God answered their prayers. In one night God sent an angel into the camp of the Assyrians and killed one hundred eighty-six thousand. So Sennacherib re-turned to his own land and while he was worshipping in his temple, his own murdered him. (He thought his god was the living God.)

Today the same thing is true. Wherever there is a recovery among God's people, there will be spiritual conflict. It will come right away. Immediately you will be surrounded by the enemy. In one sense we should do everything we can because that is our duty; but, on the other hand we know we are no match for the enemy. But, thank God, we know where to go. If we put our trust in the Lord and pray, we will find there is nothing too hard for the Lord. There will be victory.

When Hezekiah was thirty-nine years old in the prime of his life, he was sick and God sent the prophet Isaiah to him saying: "Set thy house in order; for thou shalt die, and not live." (2 Kings 20:1). God was calling him but instead of accepting God's will he wept before the Lord and said: "Ah! Jehovah, remember, I beseech thee, how I have walked before thee in truth and with a perfect heart, and have done what is good in thy sight" (2 Kings 20:3). Instead of submitting himself to the will of God he wanted to stay and enjoy the blessings of God. Because he wept much before the Lord, God's heart was touched and He sent the prophet back to heal him and give him a sign. The dial of Ahaz went back 10 degrees. A most wonderful healing and a most wonderful sign was given! It was marvelous yet it was the saddest thing that could ever happen to King Hezekiah. When his time was ripe, that should have been the time for him to go and if he should leave at that moment, what a history would be left behind—untarnished! Unfortunately he did not yield to the will of God and it was a tragedy. Dear brothers and sisters, our time is in God's hand. If our course is not finished, we will not go. We should not go.

But, if our course is finished, it would be the happiest thing for us to go.

Let's look at what Paul wrote in Philippians. At that time he was in prison in Rome waiting for Nero to give his judgment and it was possible this could be the end. So Paul said: "... and what I shall choose I cannot tell. But I am pressed by both ... departure and being with Christ ... remaining in the flesh ..." Paul would love to go because he would see Christ face to face, "... and to die is gain ..." But as he thought about the Philippians, he felt probably the Lord wanted him to stay, "... but remaining in the flesh is more necessary for your sakes ..."

During Paul's second Roman imprisonment before he was sentenced, he knew his end was coming and he wrote this to his son Timothy: "I have combated the good combat, I have finished the race, I have kept the faith. Henceforth the crown of righteousness is laid up for me, which the Lord, the righteous Judge, will render to me in that day; but not only to me, but also to all who love his appearing." (2 Timothy 4:7-8). Brothers and sisters, if our course is not finished, we will not and cannot go.

Melanchthon, the theologian of the Reformation, was of a weak constitution because he lived a very ascetic life like Timothy. One time he was literally dying and Martin Luther, who had a very strong personality, went to see him. Luther said: "You cannot die because God still needs you and in the Name of Jesus I command you to live." Well, Melanchthon lived. Brothers and sisters, our time is in God's hand and if our time is finished, let us go very gladly because we shall see the Lord. There is no reason to linger. This is the best thing that could happen to us.

So far as God was concerned Hezekiah's course was finished; but, unfortunately he didn't want to go and God yielded to him. You know, our God is not like that stern, inflexible God as many think. Our God is very soft-hearted. When Hezekiah wept before the Lord, the Lord could not stand it any more. He gave in and let Hezekiah have fifteen years more. But notice what happened within those fifteen years:

> In those days Hezekiah was sick unto death, and he prayed to Jehovah; and he spoke to him and gave him a sign. But Hezekiah rendered not again according to the benefit done to him, for his heart was lifted up; and there was wrath upon him, and upon Judah and Jerusalem. (2 Chron. 32:24-25)

Because he forced God to his will, he felt he was so strong he could force God to do what he wanted. He became proud and did not give the glory to God as before. During those fifteen years two things happened. (1) When the king of Babylon heard that he was miraculously healed, he sent messengers to him to express their sympathy. At that time Babylon was just rising up as a nation. Of course, Babylon and Assyria were enemies and Assyria was a great empire then. When the messengers of Babylon came to see Hezekiah, outwardly it was to show their joy with him; but, probably there was an ulterior motive. Hezekiah was so puffed up he showed them everything he had. God left Hezekiah to test him and he failed. Because of this God said the nation of Judah, with all the riches, would be taken into Babylonian captivity. Thank God, Hezekiah did humble himself before God and because of that, the captivity did not happen in his lifetime; but, it did happen later. (2) It was during those fifteen years that his son Manasseh was born. He succeeded his father on the throne and he was one of the most wicked kings the nation of Judah ever had.

Because of the sin of Manasseh, God was determined to destroy the nation of Judah.

Brothers and sisters, this should be a lesson to us. How we need to yield ourselves to God. If we resist His will and insist upon ours, woe to us if God gives in to us. As the Psalmist said, "Then he gave them their request, but sent leanness into their soul" (Psalm 106:15).

Hezekiah was such a good king and great leader; but, towards the end he became selfish and proud and left behind a nation that was doomed to destruction. This should be a real warning to us today!

Our Heavenly Father, there is no place for us to stand but to repent in dust and ashes. Oh, we ask Thee, Lord, that Thou wilt keep us ever humble before Thee because our eyes continuously see the Lord. Lord, we cannot be proud if we see Thee. We have to repent if we see Thee so, Lord, we do ask that Thou wilt be continuously before our eyes that we may serve Thee in humility and in meekness. Oh, Lord, we pray that we may love Thy will above all things, even above our lives and our enjoyment. Lord, we want Thy will to be done in our lives that we may serve our generation according to Thy will. We pray that before our time comes we will live and do Thy will; but, when our time is up, give us that desire to see Thy face.

We just commit one another into Thy hands. We believe Thou art doing a work among Thy people today. Thou art preparing the return of the King. Thou art restoring us. Thou art restoring that holy priesthood. Thou art restoring the spiritual sacrifices. Thou art restoring the riches in Thy body. Thou art restoring that oneness of the body of Christ. Oh, Lord, we know Thou art doing such a work and we pray we may be actively engaged in it whether in the place of leadership or in the place of support. We ask that we may work together as one.

Oh, that Thy Name may be exalted, Thy Glory manifested, that the day may come that Christ shall return and we shall be with Him forever. Oh, Lord, bless Thy people. We ask in Thy precious Name. Amen.

6—Right Leadership—King Josiah

II Chronicles 34:1-3—Josiah was eight years old when he began to reign; and he reigned thirty-one years in Jerusalem. And he did what was right in the sight of Jehovah, and walked in the ways of David his father, and turned not aside to the right hand nor to the left.

And in the eighth year of his reign, while he was yet young, he began to seek after the God of David his father; and in the twelfth year he began to purge Judah and Jerusalem from the high places, and the Asherahs, and the graven images, and the molten images.

II Chronicles 34:8—And in the eighteenth year of his reign, when he purged the land and the house, he sent Shaphan the son of Azaliah, and Maaseiah the governor of the city, and Joah the son of Joahaz the chronicler, to repair the house of Jehovah his God.

II Chronicles 34:14—And when they brought out the money that had been brought into the house of Jehovah, Hilkijah the priest found the book of the law of Jehovah by Moses.

II Chronicles 34:23-28—And she said to them, Thus saith Jehovah the God of Israel: Tell the man that sent you to me, Thus saith Jehovah: Behold, I will bring evil upon this place, and upon the inhabitants thereof, all the curses that are written in the book which they have read before the king of Judah. Because they have forsaken me, and have burned incense unto other gods, that they might provoke me to anger with all the works of their hands; therefore my fury shall be poured out upon this place, and shall not be quenched. But to the king of Judah, who sent you to inquire of Jehovah, thus shall ye say to him: Thus saith Jehovah the God of Israel touching the words which thou hast heard: Because thy heart was tender, and thou didst humble thyself before God, when thou heardest his words against this place and against the inhabitants thereof, and humbledst thyself before me, and didst rend thy garments and weep before me, I also have heard thee, saith Jehovah. Behold, I will gather thee unto thy fathers, and thou shalt be gathered to thy grave in peace; and thine eyes shall not see all the evil that I will bring upon this place, and upon the inhabitants thereof. And they brought the king word again.

We have been considering together some of the kings of the nation of Judah who were raised up by God as the right leadership to His own people and under that leadership the nation was revived, restored and recovered. The one we would like to share on this evening is King Josiah. When he came to the throne he was only eight years old, just a child.

Remember under Hezekiah there was a great recovery; but, that was completely wiped out by his wicked son Manasseh. Because of his wickedness God was determined to destroy the nation of Judah. Manasseh was taken into captivity as we read 2 Chronicles 33:11: "And Jehovah brought upon them the captains of the host of the king of Assyria, who took Manasseh with fetters, and bound him with chains of brass, and carried him to Babylon." While he was in Babylon in affliction he sought Jehovah his God and humbled himself greatly before the God of his fathers and prayed to Him. When he was in real trouble he finally humbled himself and God heard him and he was brought back to Jerusalem in his kingdom. Then Manasseh knew that Jehovah was God. In his long reign of fifty-five years he literally destroyed all that God had done through his father Hezekiah; but, in the very end he did turn to God and restore the altar. However the people still worshipped in high places. After Manasseh's death his son Amon continued in wickedness for the two years of his reign until his people finally killed him. It was then that the grandson Josiah came to the throne and he was only eight years old.

The name Josiah means "Jah heals or supports or sustains." The very name of God was in his name. Evidently he was born after his grandfather Manasseh returned to the Lord which might be the reason the name of the Lord was there. After his grandfather Manasseh returned to the Lord which might be the reason the name of the Lord was there. Josiah represents the principle of grace. So far as this little boy was concerned, what could you expect of him? What could he do to resist all the evils that had been accumulated through the years? Could he do anything to undermine the evils of the past and lead the nation in a new way. You can hardly expect a child to do such a work; but, that was the very thing Josiah did. So there is only one explanation: Towards the very end of the nation God was still most reluctant to destroy them. How God was faithful to His promise. At the very end of their history God gave them one of the best kings they ever had. That is grace.

Even though Josiah was not able to deliver the nation out of destruction or judgment; yet he did postpone God's judgment of that nation and during those days of postponement many people must have been brought back to the Lord. Now, brothers and sisters, I feel in a very broad sense that a judgment is determined upon this earth. The world is not getting better; it is getting worse. God's judgment is determined upon the land; but, even so, we can still see the grace, mercy and compassion of God. Because of the evil in this world, it should have been long consumed. Sometimes we wonder how long is the longsuffering of God. When the world is approaching its very end, the Spirit of God is moving all over this world in raising up people whose hearts are turned towards Him. These people will not be able to turn God's judgment away from the world; but, at least it postpones it and during the days of God's postponement He is able to gather unto Himself a people prepared for His return. So, brothers and sisters, we are actually living on borrowed time! It is because of the longsuffering and mercy of God that the world still continues; but, it will not be long. I believe as we study the life of Josiah we can see the grace of God at every turn.

Humanly speaking, since Josiah was a child, he would not be able to turn the tide; yet, he was raised up by God to stand against the tide and delay the flood. During the first years of his reign it seems as if nothing was done or said; but, his heart was towards the Lord. In the eighth year of his reign when he was fifteen, he began to seek after the God of David his father. Here we see the two sides of truth. On the one side there is the sovereign grace of God which is not conditioned upon anything and this grace came upon the child Josiah. Now on the other hand when he was fifteen, he began to seek the God of his father David. When grace comes upon us, it is sovereign, not depending upon who we are or what we have done or not done; but, after the grace of God has come upon us, we do have a responsibility which is how do we respond to this grace. Do we respond by seeking Him or do we respond negatively and just waste His grace? This is possible. I believe we should respond to God's grace in the way in which Josiah did.

Now who is the God of David? The God of David is more than just God. The God whom David knew and served was the God of fullness. He was not just the Creator, not just the Redeemer; but, God was everything to David. As you read the Psalms, you will see he describes the God whom he loved and served in many different ways. Sometimes you may think it is poetical; but, with David everything he said about God was a real and living experience to him. He addressed God as his rock, his fortress, his high tower, his shield, his refuge, his peace, his joy and his glory. You see that in the long experience of David he came to know God as everything to him. God was truly all in all to David and that is knowing God in fullness.

This is what you find in Ephesians 1 where Paul prays that we may be given the spirit of wisdom and revelation to the full knowledge of God, not just some knowledge of God. You know, some people as they seek God are contented with just some knowledge of the Lord. Just recently in conversation with another believer in the Lord as we were talking, the question was raised by the sister: "Why is it that many of God's people who seem to love the Lord yet in their seeking after God they appear to come to a point and no further? You would think with their love towards the Lord certainly there will be no limit; but, it looks as though they reach a point and are contented. They do not want to know more or go beyond that. For them this is enough."

How do you answer such a question? Only God knows. You do find that among God's people there are those who seek God but not in His fullness. Then there are others who never seem to be contented in their seeking after God. There is always that holy restlessness or discontentment. No matter how much God has been revealed to them, they are still seeking and stretching forth. To them God has no limit. He is infinite and because He is, the knowledge of God has no limit and they are always stretching forth. To these believers God becomes more and more. He is everything and all to them.

Josiah was just a teen-ager; but, his seeking after God was of such intensity that he wasn't satisfied with just knowing God. He wanted to know the God of David his father. Because his heart was towards God, we read this comment of the Holy Spirit concerning Josiah in II Kings 23:25:

> And like unto him was there no king before him, that turned to the Lord with all his heart, and with all his soul, and with all his might, according to all the law of Moses; neither after him arose there any like him.

He was unique; he was special! He really loved the Lord and served Him walking in His ways with all his being, not turning to the right or left doing everything right in the sight of the Lord. What a teen-ager! especially a young man in the position of king over a nation. This was most unusual. I think this should really encourage us. Sometimes we think a teen-ager can't do much so we don't expect much of them. You know, if we see a teen-ager who has a little heart for the Lord, we are more than happy. We think this is quite unusual; but, I believe we limit God. God can work in a teen-ager in the very way in which He did in Josiah.

During the twelfth year of his reign when he was twenty years old, he began to purge Judah and Jerusalem from the high places and the land from all idols. He took action. First he received grace which began to work in him and he responded by seeking the Lord with all his heart. When he was ready within, the spiritual energy began to be expressed without. As a young man of twenty he led the nation in purging the land. If you read 2 Kings and 2 Chronicles, you will see great spiritual energy demonstrated. You can read the things which he did: Purged the land, destroyed all the pillars, all the high places, all the altars, everything that his ancestor had built up—even the mount of Solomon. Solomon had a mountain where he put his idols and Josiah destroyed them all. He did a most thorough work. This extended way out from the nation of Judah to all the land of Israel because as we mentioned last night, the Northern kingdom of Israel was already destroyed by the king of Assyria. There were people left there who were probably the poorest. A vacuum was there. Josiah had such spiritual energy that the purging of the land was not limited to his own rule but extended to all of Israel.

You know, there is something very interesting in the history of Israel. When the nation was divided into the Northern and Southern kingdom very interesting in the history of Israel. When the nation was divided into the Northern and Southern kingdoms, which was about three hundred years before the time of Josiah, Jeroboam, the first king of the Northern kingdom, took the ten tribes away from Rehoboam the son of Solomon and established the nation of Israel with Samaria as the capital. He noticed that people still went to Jerusalem to worship God and he was afraid of that; so, he made two golden calves and put one in Bethel and the other in Dan. Then he told the people that they need not go to Jerusalem to worship God as He was right here in Bethel and Dan. He also proclaimed set feasts and set up priests who were not Levites. One day when he was sacrificing on the altar to the golden calf in Bethel something happened. God sent a prophet, a man of God, to Bethel from Judah and proclaimed this word:

> And behold, there came a man of God from Judah, by the word of Jehovah, to Bethel; and Jeroboam stood by the altar to burn incense. And he cried against the altar by the word of Jehovah, and said, O altar, altar! thus saith Jehovah: Behold, a child shall born unto the house of David, Josiah by name; and upon thee shall he sacrifice the priests of the high places that burn incense upon thee, and men's bones shall be burned upon thee. And he gave a sign the same day, saying, This is the sign that Jehovah hath spoken: Behold, the altar shall be rent, and the ashes that are upon it shall be poured out. (I Kings 13:1-3)

Now remember this was over three hundred years before King Josiah; but, we see how he purged the land not only in Judah but even in the Northern kingdom. The way in which he did it was to desecrate all the altars. He not only destroyed the altars but he burned the bones of the priests of these idols upon the altar. If you read the description of 2 Kings, you will find this literally happened.

Then there is the story about this man of God who did not listen to God's word and was deceived by the old prophet. He was killed by the lion and buried there in

Bethel. The old prophet then asked his sons to bury him beside this prophet because when all the bones were dug up and Josiah would look back and say: "What tombstone is that which I see? And the men of the city told him, It is the sepulcher of the man of God who came from Judah and proclaimed these things which thou hast done against the altar of Bethel. And he said, Let him alone; let no man move his bones."

There was such spiritual energy in that young man, Josiah. He was able to purge the whole land and made all Israel to worship God. You know, in the family of God there are children, young people and fathers. In 1 John chapter 2 you find the children know the father. When we are born again, the Holy Spirit bears witness with our spirit and cries out, Abba Father; but, the young men are characterized by spiritual strength and energy. "I have written to you, young men, because ye are strong, and the word of God abides in you, and ye have overcome the wicked one" (1 John 2:14). Young men should demonstrate the spiritual energy and strength of the Lord, not natural zeal, but spiritual strength to overcome the world.

In the Scriptures you see how God raised up and used many young people. It is true, spiritual maturity does take time. You cannot have instant spirituality; yet God did use many young people such as Joseph, Joshua, David, Samuel, Daniel, Jeremiah and in the New Testament, John, Timothy, Mark—all so young. If a person is apprehended by the Lord when he is young, he is delivered from many sins and sorrows and there is more time for God to mature and use him. So young people should not draw back. Of course, there is something to be afraid of and that is natural zeal and energy which knows almost no bounds. If we know the

Lord when we are young, there will be spiritual energy and strength demonstrated such as we see in Josiah.

When Josiah was twenty-five after he had done such a thorough work of purging the land and repairing the house of God, the book of the law was discovered in the temple. Think of that! According to the law when a new king came to the throne, a copy of the law should be given to him that he might meditate upon it day and night in order to do the right thing. Evidently after the reign of Manasseh, the whole thing was completely unknown. There was not even the book of the law. As a matter of fact it was out of Josiah's communion with God that he was inspired to do all of these things and without the proper guidance of the book. When the book of the law was discovered, it was most likely Deuteronomy that was read because when the words were read, Josiah rent his garments. In other words, in Deuteronomy God said if you forsake me and worship idols, I will scatter you all over the world and the curses will come upon you. All of these things happened.

Josiah sent people to seek the prophetess Huldah to inquire of the Lord. You know, the prophet Jeremiah began to prophesy in the thirteenth year of King Josiah. Now Josiah and Jeremiah were both young people at this time and their hearts must have been closely intertwined. They worked together—Josiah on the throne and Jeremiah as a prophet supporting this work of recovery. It is strange that Josiah would send for Huldah and not Jeremiah. Also Zephaniah was prophesying at the same time; but he did not inquire of him. This is very strange and I do not pretend to know why. This was a most unusual time. God used a child to lead a nation and He spoke through a prophetess instead of a prophet. Maybe the Lord lead Josiah in that way. I don't know; but, at least Josiah was open to whatever channel God may use. Huldah told him that the judgment could not be averted—the judgment of the Lord was determined. Because the heart of Josiah was tender and he trembled at God's word, God promised him it would not happen in his lifetime. In other words it was postponed.

Remember when God told Hezekiah to prepare to go; he wept before God because he wanted to live on and enjoy the blessings. Hezekiah did not yield under the will of God but presented all the good things he had done for God. The result was tragic. Now Josiah, when the word of God was read, could have done the same thing; but, he did not think highly of himself. He humbled himself before the Lord and bowed under the mighty hand of God. Dear brothers and sisters, this is something for us to consider. How important it is that we learn to bow under the mighty hand of God and if we do this, in due time He will exalt us.

Josiah not only had the inward leading from the Lord, he had the word of God in his hand. With these two things he doubled his efforts in serving God. He called the whole nation to come for a Passover which was something that was not done for a long time. During the days of Hezekiah they had the Passover; but, it wasn't done exactly according to law because they didn't keep it in the first month which was the proper time. As we see here, Josiah, with the word of God guiding him, was able to return everything to the original design of God. It was a mighty recovery! Whenever there is a recovery of such a degree, there will always be the combination of these two things: The leading of the Spirit and the guidance of the word. Some people emphasize so much on the inward leading that they neglect the word of God. Others, who are so literal in the letter of the word, fail to know the leading of the Spirit within. When you find an imbalance here, you won't be able to get into the fullness of God's way.

Josiah was on the throne for thirty-one years and it was during that time that Necho, King of Egypt, came up to fight against the king of Assyria. You know, the nation of Judah was so situated that it became the battlefield between the north and the south. You have the Egyptian empire in the south and the Assyrian empire in the north and any conflict between these two great empires would involve Judah being the passway between the lands. It is almost unbelievable that Josiah would go out against the king of Egypt without inquiring of the Lord. There is no mentioning that he did. Actually the king of Egypt was not against him but just passing through. Somehow Josiah became frightened and was presumptuous. Probably after God had blessed him in such a way, he felt secure and strong about it and instead of inquiring of the Lord, he just went forward to fight against the king of Egypt. Humanly speaking that was impossible because Egypt was a great empire; but, Josiah must have presumed God was with him and would deliver him from the hand of Necho. God even used the mouth of the king of Egypt to warn Josiah; but, he did not listen. Necho emphasized that God told him this word:

> I come not against thee this day, but against the house with which I have war; and God has told me to make haste: keep aloof from God who is with me, that he destroy thee not. (II Chronicles 35:21)

Notice that within Josiah there was something which was not quite right because he disguised himself and in his presumption he went out and was killed. In one sense I think probably he did commit the sin of presumption. You remember in Psalm 19 the prayer there in verse 12 and onward:

> Who understandeth his errors? Purify me from secret faults. Keep back thy servant also from presumptuous sins; let them not have dominion over me: then shall I be perfect, and I shall be innocent from great transgression. Let the words of my mouth and the meditation of my heart be acceptable in thy sight, O Jehovah, my rock, and my redeemer. (Psalm 19:12-14)

There are presumptuous sins. You do not really seek the Lord or know what His will is; but, you presume that it must be so. We need to ask the Lord to keep us back from presumptuous sins. Nothing is to be taken for granted. We need to humble ourselves before the Lord in everything; then we will be delivered from great transgressions.

God overruled this matter because He used the opportunity (even though it might not have been God's direct will) to take His servant away so he could not see what would happen to the nation. In other words God kept His word, His promise. Brothers and sisters, this is something beyond our understanding. We are not in any position to say this was the time which Josiah should go or whether, because of his being presumptuous, he went earlier than he should have. We do not know. We can only say God overruled and made it good. Here is where we need to be careful before the Lord, especially when we know the presence and the blessing of the Lord. This is the time when we should ask the Lord to keep us from being presumptuous; then God's time will not be cut short in any way.

Thank God! our situation is different from Josiah's. With him he was not able to turn away the wrath or judgment of God. He was able to postpone it and God took him away by death so he might not see the things that would happen to the nation. In our case we are not to be taken away by death but our hope is that we may be raptured alive. We know judgment is coming to this world soon. That will not change; it may postpone; but it will come! Our blessed hope is that we may be taken away by rapture. This is what you will find promised to the church in Philadelphia. To those who overcome the promise of the Lord is: "Because thou hast kept the word of my patience, I also will keep thee out of the hour of trial, which is about to come upon the whole habitable world to try them that dwell upon the earth" (Revelation 3:10). The trial, of course, means the Great Tribulation. When judgment is really poured forth upon this earth, our Lord does promise there will be people who shall escape and not see this judgment because they are taken to the throne.

So, dear brothers and sisters, let us take this as our blessed hope.

Our Heavenly Father, we do pray that in these last of last days that our hearts may be towards Thee just as Thy servant Josiah that we might walk in Thy ways and seek Thee with all our hearts, all our soul and all our strength. Oh, that we may do right in Thy sight not turning to the right or the left. May we be used of Thee to bring in recovery to the land, to Thy people, to worship. Lord, we pray that we may never commit the sin of presumption but always walk softly before Thee throughout our lives.

Oh, Lord, our hope is that Thou wilt take us to Thyself even before judgment is poured forth upon this earth. Thou hast promised it and we pray that by Thy grace it will come to us. It is all for Thy praise and glory. We ask in Thy precious Name. Amen.

www.ingramcontent.com/pod-product-compliance
Lightning Source LLC
Chambersburg PA
CBHW071903020426
42331CB00010B/2647